Jean Inglis Lincoln

NOBODY HOME
a memoir

JACQUELINE MASUMIAN

ACKNOWLEDGEMENTS

Many people assisted me with this project. First on the list is Gail Howard, who encouraged me to explore the person my mother was and helped me extract so many memories I'd thought were dormant. My band of fellow memoir writers, Lyn Garson, Kim Prario, LuAnne Roy, Jim Nixon, Kevin Clark, and Norma and George Schofield deserve much praise for listening and helping me shape the narrative in its early stages. Heartfelt thanks go to Jessica Bram for her wisdom, intuitiveness, and valuable editing, as well as to Suzanne Hoover for her thoughtful comments. Kathy Van der Aue, Patricia Chadwick, Diana Weller, Jody Foote, Kathy Serocki, and Sheila Traub gave invaluable feedback. And Marcelle Soviero provided excellent remarks on the text, as well as inspiration for publishing. I am grateful to my cousin Blair Morton who, after reading a late draft, set me straight on a few crucial facts. I'm also indebted to other family members who helped me keep the details accurate when my memory was playing tricks on me. Additionally, they provided reminders of bits of my mother's humor that had escaped me entirely. Thanks to my readers, Linda Fitzgerald, Julie Monahan, and Nancy McCormick who gave me direction and moral support. And to Barbara L. Smith for her careful editing and enthusiasm for the project. Many friends gave me an occasional boost when I needed it; they know who they are. Most of all I thank my wonderful George who saw me through the entire process, listening, reading, and reading again.

To Marjorie
To my darling George
And to my mom

1

LETTERS

Today is the 16th of April, my mother's birthday. It's a date I never forget, though she's been dead for over twenty years. As is my custom on this day, I take a few moments to focus my thoughts on her. I gaze out my picture window into the garden beyond and wonder, who was this woman who raised me?

I used to think she was like Katherine Hepburn with her independent spirit, her strength and wit. But there was another side to her, the Joan Crawford side, dark and angry. As I muse on my mother, trying to pull together a clear picture of who she was, I realize my memories of her are nothing more than a ragged patchwork of words and images and places of my childhood. They are nothing substantial, merely pieces.

My mother was an individual who—it appeared to her children—considered her life a tragedy. When she died, I felt sad, not that she was gone, but that she had been miserable for so much of her existence. From time to time—in therapy or out—I have clawed away at scattered bits of dubious memory to try to explain her. But this year, on this day, for some unknown reason, I feel a need for something more. I want something tangible to bring her closer to me, to help validate those memories and make sense of them. *Letters*, I think, *there must be letters.*

I pull open my desk drawer and extract the battered manila file folder I've labeled "*Family Letters, Info.*" But as I leaf through it, I discover to my amazement that I have not saved a single letter from my mother. I have nothing—no letters, no notes, no photos. The folder holds annotated newspaper clippings from my older sister Marian, thank-you notes from my younger sister Holly, and photos and child-script notes from my godson Jamie. There is also a photocopy of a letter from my father, written in studied cursive by his caretaker, stating his wishes for the time of his death. But I have not one thing written in my mother's hand.

Her letters were remarkable; it's curious there are none here. I cast my eyes around my untidy home office, trying to think where else I might have stored them. Surely her letters are here somewhere.

My mother was a prolific letter writer, a master of that now nearly lost art. When I was away at college, she wrote on stationery with her name embossed at the top, "Jean Inglis Lincoln." When off in Europe or the Caribbean, she sent me missives on thin pale blue writing paper bearing the name of the hotel where she was staying. Many years later, when I had moved away from home, she wrote to me on designer note cards decorated with details from famous landscape paintings.

Each letter from her began with a caustic complaint about the weather—the Cleveland climate being to her synonymous with misery—then moved on to a witty recounting of news from our rural home outside the city. She often ended the letters with an offer of money—"if you need it"—or a line such as, "Since I cannot think of a single piece of scintillating news, I shall close here. Love, Mom."

Her letters were entertaining—apart from the complaints about the weather—and it's inconceivable that I wouldn't have saved even one of them. Did I toss each one after reading it, digesting its contents, and meeting my obligation to reply? Did I save them but decide to throw bunches of them out as I moved from place to place? Was I furious with her at some point and decide to pitch anything she'd ever written me? Or did I merely come to see her letters as expendable clutter and discard them?

I now long for those letters. I finger through some other folders in the drawer hoping to come across a card or note from her, but there are no missives of any kind. Could I really have been so careless as to lose them? If I could find a sample of my mother's writing, I would feel I truly held a piece of her, something I seem to need right now.

With a growing sense of urgency, I glance around my office. I have inherited some of her beautiful, though battered, antique furniture, and hanging on my wall are paintings and etchings she gave me as gifts over the years. These objects surround me every day and connect me to the homes of my childhood. But to have none of her letters alarms me.

I yearn to see her unique handwriting. She wrote not in cursive, but in printing the letters of which were each separate and distinct, featuring beautiful curves. It was an italics of sorts. Her *h*'s and *k*'s were tall and proud with lovely loops, her *i*'s were upright squiggles, her *m*'s had small curls beyond their humps. It's as though my mother had invented her very own style of handwriting, elegant but disjointed.

Her style of mothering was her own invention, as well. She was nothing like anybody else's mom. My friends' mothers went to hairdressers and country clubs. They took their children to cultural events and shopping, arranged birthday parties, and mended clothes. I don't remember my mother doing any of those things during my childhood. Her maternal moments were somewhat random, disordered, disconnected from the woman she may have longed to be.

But perhaps my memory is faulty. Maybe she did in fact do at least some of those motherly things, but I was unaware—too caught up in my childish self—and the incidences of her maternal care have now vanished from my consciousness. Or possibly they have been overshadowed by the cheerless times I do recall.

In any event, she was my mother, the source of all that I am. Every event of my life has been caught up in the stream of her words, her interests, her actions, and her needs. I have been successful, I believe, in taking charge of my own life, and yet at times I feel I am little but a product of her. She is certainly the key to any insight I might have now or in the future as to who I am. So I must find her letters.

I wrap a sturdy rubber band around the worn manila folder "*Family Letters, Info*" and reluctantly file it away in the left-hand drawer of my desk. There are no letters here, and this is the only place I can think to look. But I am not satisfied. I search once again around my messy office, opening and shutting drawers, rifling through a closet full of photos. Where else, I wonder, with a growing sense of desperation, where else can I find something—anything at all—written in her distinctive hand?

2

THE PHOTOGRAPH

The letters do not present themselves. And since she rarely let us take her picture, always managing to dodge our Kodaks, there are no snapshots of my mother, either. But there is one thing.

I stare at the photo of my sister Marian's christening from 1937. It depicts my grandparents, my mother's parents, posing in the rear yard of their handsome house in Lyndhurst, Ohio, where the blocks of stone and the dark wood siding are graced with hollyhocks seven feet tall. My grandmother, wearing a silk print dress, faces the camera with an air of reserve, while my grandfather handles the pipe he's been smoking. Next to them is my Aunt Marian who is flirting girlishly with the camera, and Uncle Doug, her husband, standing at the rear. The Episcopal priest Father Peterson, rotund and holding himself a bit apart from the family, offers a mild tight-lipped grin. And the infant, the baby Marian, peers out from her christening dress with coal-black eyes, questioning the world into which she has been born.

But central to the photo are two unhappy looking young people. My mother, her jaw a muddle of scars, forces the merest suggestion of an anxious smile and stares blankly at the camera. My father, holding the baby girl, looks down at the child, his head drawn back from her ever so slightly. Doubt clouds his face. This is the beginning of our family.

The christening photograph sits amongst other pictures of pets, parents, and relatives, on the spinet piano in my living room. We often admire this photo, my siblings and I, because it depicts our grandparents' house of which we have so many vivid memories—holidays and sunny summer afternoons spent in the security of their prosperous, orderly household. And because it is a portrait of family members, all of whom, with the exception of the baby, are now lost to us. We each have a copy of the prized photograph framed simply and sitting somewhere in our respective homes.

But none of the people in this 1937 photo has an inkling of how their lives will play out beyond this moment. Their only thought is for getting the proper pose for the photographer, so the event shall be recorded for all time.

Two years after my sister Marian's birth my parents will have a son, David. Seven years later, following World War II, I will enter the world, and soon my younger sister Holly will be born. Two years beyond this assemblage of children my parents' marriage will end in a bitter divorce. And finally, my mother's sister Marian will die, leaving behind two young girls who will come to live with us.

We will all be cut adrift from the possibility of the traditional family one viewing this photograph might have expected. And so our story begins.

3
FRAGMENTS

Oh, we ain't got a barrel of money,

Maybe we're ragged and funny,

But we're travelin' along

Singin' a song

Side by side.

From some deep place this memory emerges. My mother and her two little girls, Holly and I, are standing in a circle holding hands, swinging our arms and singing "Side by Side." Giggling hysterically as we sing, our eyes squinty with glee, our pink mouths gleaming on a bright summer day.

Who knows where this memory comes from, but it is a pleasing one. Just one happy little family, singing, playing a game like "Ring Around the Rosie." But where's my father? And why are we singing about not having a barrel of money and being ragged and funny?

An earlier recollection: I am a toddler and my father is putting me to bed.

"When will I see you again, Daddy? Tomorrow?"

"No, not tomorrow."

"The day after tomorrow?" I ask.

"No, no, not the day after tomorrow, dear."

"Well, when?"

"The day after the day after the day after the day after the day after the day after tomorrow," he replies.

The repetition of the phrase tickles me, and I repeat it after him. "The day after the day after . . ." But it seems a long time. And why is my daddy living somewhere else?

And so, my mother was left alone with two little girls as well as two older children, Marian and David, in a big white house with wide fluted columns flanking the front door and a sunny grape arbor in the back yard overlooking the golf course.

And then we moved—to a black house with tall trees casting shadows onto the lawn. Perhaps we moved because my mother didn't have a barrel of money and was maybe feeling a bit ragged and anything but funny. And that's where we sang "Side by Side"— at the black house—not at the big white house, after all.

There was other silliness from the early days when we were little. In the evening, when Holly and I resisted going to bed, our mom chased us around the upstairs hall shouting, "If you girls don't behave, I'll throw you in the garbage can! Garbage can!" Holly and I skittered around screaming with maniacal baby laughter, taunting her to play the game more and more. "Garbage can! Garbage can!"

Another nighttime game we played: Holly and I decide to compete to be the first up and dressed in the morning; we climb into our little beds partially clothed, to give ourselves a head start, and to win.

And playing Scrabble with Mommy at the living room coffee table. My lucky "Z" on a Triple Word Score served up with a guilty burble of joy, for victory.

But best was the "Side by Side" game with our mom, laughing and swinging our arms back and forth. I can think of very few other times we three sang and held hands. None, in fact. But I know we laughed together over the years to come. My mother had a talent for delivering a clever remark, an off-beat joke that would make us giggle. So, we laughed when we were youngsters, we did that. Sometimes. But what did we laugh about? I cannot remember.

> *"Oh, we ain't got a barrel of money . . ."*

The tune spins around in my brain,

> *"Travelin' along, singin' a song,"*

as I seek some semblance of a family

> *"Side by side."*

4

SANCTUARY

I peered down the woodsy slope. Through the shade of the trees, water flickered at the bottom of the ravine. I wanted to get closer.

I was eight and we had moved again, from the black house on the tree-lined streets of Shaker Heights to a stately home in rural Gates Mills. We needed a larger house because my aunt Marian had died and left behind my two cousins, Jeanie and Susan, who were to come live with us. The new house could accommodate us all.

Gates Mills, sitting on the banks of the Chagrin River, was the home of the Chagrin Valley Hunt Club, destination of the horsy set. My grandmother had bought horses for my sister Marian and my cousin Jeanie, and they'd begun to ride regularly and compete in local horseshows, so this little town with its club and tavern and pristine white Episcopal church was to be our new address.

My mother, probably with the help of our grandparents, bought the West Hill Drive house, a large white colonial with nine bedrooms, including servants' quarters. It seemed quite grand to us with its airy entry hall, generous formal living and dining rooms, and huge kitchen with an old-fashioned icebox built into one wall.

Located at the end of a long gravel driveway, the handsome structure was surrounded on three sides by a bit of lawn and garden
beyond which lay acres of steep wooded ravines.

At eight, I was perhaps too young to learn to ride, but I longed
to be outdoors. Which is how I found myself one spring day, peering down the intriguing slope on the north side of our yard. What's
down there, I thought. I scrabbled down, sliding on my rear end,
grabbing onto saplings, getting an occasional foothold on a rock,
and finally finding my way to the brook some thirty feet below.

Once down, I scanned the scene; it was disappointingly dark
and damp. A stream, yes, but nothing else but dead leaves and twigs.
Cold water was seeping into my sneakers. I surveyed the steep
incline I had descended and realized I now had to find my way back
up.

I started to hoist myself, grasping at stones, then sliding down
in the wet dirt, climbing up a few feet, then falling back again.
Clumps of black mud tumbled down with me. The saplings proved
too weak to hold my weight, the soil too fragile, the rocks too slick
and unsteady. I moved downstream hoping to find better footing
there. After numerous attempts, my head buzzed with alarm. I had
visions of needing to cry for help, though I knew my siblings were off
and about and my mother was quietly reading her book inside the
house, oblivious to my whereabouts. Looking to my right, I waded
upstream, found an area that was less steep, and finally scrambled
my way out of the ravine and onto the safety of our lawn. Covered in
muck, I lay on the clean grass, panting and feeling a fool.

Shortly after this misadventure, I found a spot on the other side
of the yard that enchanted me. A rough grassy area led into a stand
of tall trees, some of them evergreens. Once into the woodland, I
picked my way along the suggestion of a path until the house, the

driveway, and the open area were out of sight. Through a canopy of dark green leaves high above, rays of sunlight stretched to the leafy soil at my feet. I stood among giant tree trunks, woodland grasses and ferns embracing my shins, and lifted my head to look up through the branches. A dart of sunlight found my eye, blinding me till I shifted my gaze to patches of blue sky.

The ground to my left edged gently down to a small stream. I crouched amidst mossy stones, ferns, and ragged groundcover and stared at the trickling water. Grasping a sturdy stick, I pulled clumps of soggy leaves away from the streambed allowing the water to run more freely. It raced over and around small rocks and pebbles and cascaded to the ravine below. Sunlight glistened on the brook amidst the intricate patterns of the ferns and the clean fragrance of moist humus.

Soon a world beyond this place did not exist for me; I was lost in the spell of my new-found home. In this secluded spot I was removed from the unease spurred by my mother's often anxious voice. There was no one here whose mood I had to judge. There was no worry that I might make a mistake and say the wrong thing. And no insecurity about whether I was a blessing or a burden. The earth and trees and sky were ordered just as they should be; they managed themselves serenely. They watched over and sheltered me.

Beyond the stream, I walked deeper into the woods, dry leaves and twigs rustling beneath my feet. Soon I came to a small clearing. There I found a rotted tree stump surrounded by a perfect circle of white-capped mushrooms and tufts of bushy grass. I knew it immediately to be a fairy ring. According to my books, this was where the fairies danced at night, singing and cavorting in a merry circle. At eight I was too old to believe in fairies, and yet, I could easily imagine their gatherings. Beyond the fairy ring lay more woods, more cool darkness.

I spent many spring and summer days in my forest, always by myself. Holly had no interest in the woods, and that was fine; I wanted no one with me. In my private retreat I could watch the seasons and weather patterns come and go. I found breezy days best, leafy branches swaying above me. As I traipsed along, I imagined myself as a female Daniel Boone, breaking twigs and trampling down leaves to make trails. I regularly checked on my stream, clearing away any debris that had collected, making sure the water flowed unimpeded. I visited my fairy ring looking for any signs of recent activity. And I continued to create new paths where none had been.

One afternoon Holly was at a friend's house, and my mother had to go out. "I'll be back soon, Jack," she said. The cleaning lady Nettie was there to mind me, but she was busy with her ironing. With nobody home, I found the house especially big and empty, so I went to my leafy sanctuary. I sat cross-legged at the edge of the fairy ring, feeling the warm sun on my back. I breathed in the damp, pungent air. I was content, solitary, with daydreams my only company.

I whiled away a long afternoon there, but then realized I hadn't heard my mother's car on the gravel drive—she'd been gone far longer than she said she'd be. I tramped through the ferns to the driveway that passed alongside the woods and waited for her. It seemed a long time. Finally, I saw her car heading toward me. She stopped and rolled down her window. Her short wavy hair brushed up and back from her face gave her an insouciant air. Wherever she'd been, it had put her in a good mood. "Jack, you're out here all alone!" she laughed. "Such a good girl—waiting 'like patience on a monument.'" She chortled at her clever quote, rolled up the window, and drove on to the house.

I stood and watched as she drove away. I was by myself again. The sky had turned gray and empty. I made my way back to the forest. Simple and protective, it drew me in and held me till dinnertime.

5
THE LAMB

The house on West Hill Drive was a remote, sometimes lonely, place. Our cousin Eric had dubbed it "Bleak House" because, as he had discovered on a number of visits, everybody there seemed to be in a dark mood, withdrawn, bored, and grumbling.

The long gravel driveway was a prominent feature of the property. Running a quarter of a mile through the woods, it looped around in front of the house to encircle a stretch of meager lawn under two enormous beech trees. The deep shade in the yard provided a sense of perpetual doom.

We could view the rutted strip of gravel from the window seat at the front stairway landing. Holly and I, two quiet youngsters, would sit there for hours either reading or gazing along the length of the driveway, hoping for the approach of someone or something to relieve our tedium. We developed what we called the "looking-down-the-driveway disease," a fixation on that driveway and what might lie beyond or who might possibly stop by for a visit to enliven our endlessly drab day.

There were few neighborhood children to play with. Even those next door lived a quarter of a mile up our driveway and along a wide road lined with wildflower fields. We had bikes, but they, even when the tires weren't deflated or the chains fallen off, were difficult to maneuver on the pothole-ridden gravel. So Holly and I, far too shy to seek out friends in any event, puttered around home with nothing to do. At times we stomped around the house singing, to the tune of "Here Comes the Bride," "Nothing to do, nothing to do, dah-dah-duh-dah-dah, nothing to do!"

One muggy summer morning my mother, seated on the living room couch reading *Please Don't Eat the Daisies*, plumbed her imagination for some project to get us out of the house. "Why don't you go out and see if you can fix the leak in the pond, girls?"

The so-called pond, a tiny concrete bowl carved out of the back yard landscape, had at some time perhaps held goldfish. We'd painted it a vivid blue the previous year, but now a huge crack coursed through the cement, and any water that might have collected had leaked away, making the pond virtually unusable for fish or anything else.

Following our mother's suggestion, Holly and I traipsed out to the pond, cleared away all the damp leaves and sticks, and tried to wedge something—glue or putty or chewing gum, perhaps—into the wavering crack. After a hasty attempt at this task, I said, "That looks pretty good. Let's give it a try."

"No, it doesn't," said Holly, scowling. "You can still see most of the crack."

"Well, it's good enough," I retorted, impatient to have the futile project done.

We filled the pond with water from the garden hose to see if our patch would hold. It didn't, not completely, but we enjoyed bathing our feet for a while, till the cool water seeped away.

One spring my mother came up with another idea to keep us amused. While some mothers gave their children cute yellow chicks or white rabbits as Easter gifts, ours was not content with something so pedestrian.

On Easter morning after Holly and I woke to the overflowing baskets the Easter bunny had left at the foot of our beds, my mother called us downstairs. "Go see what's in the garage, girls." We stepped through the door to the garage. Tied to the door handle of our Chevy station wagon was a baby lamb.

"Baaaa!" the little creature cried as we petted and fondled its pure white curls. It looked at us with black button eyes, and its pink ears perked.

"Thanks, Mom!" Holly and I cried, caressing our new baby.

"I thought it would be a good way to keep the lawn trimmed," she replied, grinning at her bit of whimsy. "Now, you girls have to take care of it. I think it can get by on just grass." She barked a quick laugh. "At least I hope so."

She left us to our petting and caressing. "Baaa!" cried our new friend.

Our family had had other pets, various dogs and cats and parrots, but the cats had been banished to the basement, and the other animals had all disappeared for one reason or another. So this pet, chosen just for Holly and me, was a treat. We patted the soft white wool and buried our noses to inhale the sweet skin. But soon we realized we were craving breakfast and Easter candy. We took the rope and tied our little pet to the bare trunk of a ragged hemlock tree. "Baaa!"

The lamb proved to be a darling creature that grazed on the lawn and bleated and littered the landscape with piles of sheep droppings. We found the little brown pellets intriguing at first, until their pervasive odor became repugnant.

After a few days Holly and I became weary of having to tie the lamb up and listen to its bleating all night, and we had no fenced-in area on the property, so we decided to shelter our pet in the bunk-house. A large wooden shed with a plank floor and two musty bunk beds along one wall, it had been built in the woods presumably for outdoor overnights. Holly and I had actually slept there a few times, but it had proved to be damp and spidery, so we soon lost interest in it.

However, it seemed a perfect place to house our lamb. So every night we led the animal out to the shed and shut it away. In time, the floor of the bunkhouse became carpeted in smelly sheep poop. But we didn't care —we never slept out there anymore.

The lamb often tried to follow us into the house, but my mother insisted. "No lambs in the house!"

"But Mom, —"

"I have *spoken!*" she declared in her mock imperious voice that always made us laugh.

Later we could hear the lamb bleating out in the yard as we bounced around the living room, trying to distract my mother from her reading.

"Girls, you have this entire huge house to be in! Why do you have to be right *here*?" It was true, we did have a big home full of rooms to play in and explore. But here we were, as close to our mother as we could get.

"Go out and play with your lamb, girls!" she said, her voice on edge. So we went out and chased the animal around the yard and screamed with laughter as it gamboled about from place to place. Then we went back inside to find something else to do. "Baaa!" cried the lamb, all alone.

My mother, though she had joined the church in the village and kept busy with volunteer jobs, had made few friends in the neighborhood, so that summer she treated herself to an early summer cocktail party, inviting all her Cleveland friends out to lovely Gates Mills. Among the guests were the recently divorced Mrs. Hawgood, the church organist Mr. Blodgett, and our imperious Aunt Priscilla.

The guests arrived and wandered about the house with their drinks, then settled themselves on the living room couches to sample hors d'oeuvres set out on coffee tables—salted nuts, little triangle sandwiches, and a specialty that was all the rage, chocolate-covered ants. Aunt Priscilla popped one of the dark brown morsels into her mouth. "Intriguing!" she declared and reached for another.

Just then the lamb, who had found the front door ajar, made its way through the entry hall and into the noisy living room and presented itself at Aunt Priscilla's elbow. "Baaa!" it cried. Aunt Priscilla, still munching on the chocolate-covered ants, turned to find herself nose-to-nose with our pet.

She peered at the party crasher. "Oh, Jean, dear," she said to my mother in her seriocomic voice, "who's this? Anyone we know?" The guests howled with laughter, and the lamb bleated, depositing onto the carpet what bore an alarming resemblance to chocolate-covered ants. More hilarity ensued as Holly dragged the lamb out the front door, and I dashed to grab a broom and dustpan.

Over the next few months our sweet-smelling white baby lamb morphed into a burly beige sheep. My mother had apparently anticipated neither its growth nor its needing to be sheared. Over the summer we girls lost all interest in the smelly creature, and the lawn, which my mother had expected to be neatly trimmed by the animal's grazing, had become a patchwork of weeds, bald spots, and sheep scat.

One fall afternoon Holly and I came home from school to find our wooly friend had disappeared. I never asked what had become of it. I presumed it had gone to a happier home—a place more accommodating than Bleak House.

6

THE TREAT

It's Friday afternoon, and Laurel School for Girls lets out early—at 3:00 instead of the usual 3:45. Holly and I jump into the little lavender Peugeot, a gift from my mother the day I turned sixteen. I wrestle it into gear and off we drive.

On our way home we stop at Woolworth's for our special pre-weekend treat. Inside the store we make a cursory walk around, perusing the Cover Girl makeup, the glitzy jewelry and filmy scarves. Then we zero in on what we really came for. At the candy counter large glass bins provide a splendid display—malted milk balls, spice drops, jellybeans, and our favorite—M&M's.

Knowing Holly is far too shy to order, I press my finger onto the glass front of the M&M bin. I take a deep breath. "May we have a half a pound of M&M's, please?" I ask the sales lady.

I turn to Holly. She's scowling beneath her fringe of bangs.

"No, wait, may we have a pound, please?" I correct myself.

"A pound?" the lady asks, lifting an eyebrow.

"Yes, a pound. Please."

I check Holly's lightened expression as the lady measures the glistening candy onto a scale and pours the contents into a white paper bag. My mouth waters. I pay, and we head for home, the luscious delicacy on the car seat between us.

As teens we have adopted this Friday afternoon ritual. I am relieved on those days to see Holly in a jovial mood as the two of us pop the colorful M&M's into our mouths, schoolwork and the stresses of home life forgotten for the moment. It's just the two of us, free.

Holly and I had always been known as "the babies," because we were ten years younger than Marian and David. As we were growing up our older siblings seemed to be hardly ever at home. They were either away at boarding school or college, or they were married and out of the house altogether. The same was true of our cousins, Jeanie and Susan. So for the most part it was just the "babies" who were left at home with our mother.

The way we four siblings evolved, how we adopted the roles we each came to play, has always intrigued me. Marian, the eldest, was the model child, the perfect teenager. Her senior year she had the honor of being elected May Queen at Hathaway Brown School. Eight-millimeter footage from 1954 captured her on May Day, as she paraded around the school lawns dressed in a white hoop-skirted gown, surrounded by a bevy of attendants. Her skirt bobbed back and forth as Marian walked along, smiling nervously at the assembled crowd of admiring parents, grandparents and siblings. Atop her perfect dark pageboy her attendants placed a crown of flowers.

Marian won ribbons riding in regional horse shows, she was an excellent tennis player and a beautiful debutante. She graduated magna cum laude from Smith. And some years later, while raising four children, she earned a Ph.D. and became a college professor.

David, two years younger than Marian, was a math genius and prep school football star. But he was also a brother with a mean streak and a penchant for pranks. He and his friends liked to drive around the elegant Shaker Square shopping center with the trunk of their car ajar and one of the boys lying inside with a limp arm hanging out. David would stop the car and ask passersby, "Hey, where's the dump?" One horrified shopper, eying the dangling arm, replied, "Who—I mean—*what* do you want to dump?" The boys sped off, howling with laughter.

Living with David was like inhabiting a Chas Addams cartoon, as he reveled in inflicting pain on his two little sisters. Like the time he threw a dart into Holly's leg. And the day he made me stand in a puddle of water in the basement and plug in our old wringer washing machine to see if I would get a shock. He stood and watched as I yelped in pain, then smiled and walked away. He also took delight in subjecting us to Chinese Rope Burn and Tickling Death.

Fearing his ragged moods Holly and I became his little serfs. In summer months David would raid Henry's General Store for as many little red rubber balls as he could get his hands on, then insist we play with him. "Hol, Jacq, watch this!" He proceeded to display his skill at batting the balls from our front lawn high over the house into the back woods.

"OK, kids, now go get them!"

"What?"

"Go on! Go get them, so we can do it again!"

Holly and I, eager to please, ran off to do his bidding. We searched through the woods, combing through leaf litter and fallen branches, retrieving as many as we could find, then returned panting, balls in hand, so David could hit them over the house again and again until at last all were hopelessly lost.

On summer nights after dinner, if he was in a decent mood, David drove us to the Dairy Queen where he treated us to huge banana splits. Other times he let us read his stash of MAD Magazines. For some reason, perhaps because of those generous acts or because he was the only male in the household, he had tremendous power over his little sisters.

But there were times Holly and I cringed as he and my mother argued about his shirking of household chores. David apparently saw no reason he should help; such work was beneath him.

"You're just like your father. You won't do a thing for me!" she cried.

"Why should I?" he fired back, "I can't stand this place!" The shouting match ended with David stomping out and peeling up the driveway in our Chevy station wagon. Later that summer he went to live with Dad, to be out of the house and away from her.

Then there were the two of us "babies." Holly, my little sister, was not only extremely shy; she also had a volatile temper. One day when she was about eight, she was so peeved with my mother's complaints about the impossibility of managing the household—"I can't cope," she seemed to be telling us time and time again, "Don't ask me to be a mother!"—Holly decided to run away from home. "I can't take it anymore!" she blubbered through her tears. She wrapped a few belongings into a bundle and trudged away up the long gravel driveway.

I stood on the lawn and called after her, "Come on, Hol, it's not that bad!" She plodded on. An hour or two later I was relieved to see her return home, looking defeated; she'd realized there was no place for her to go on West Hill Drive. My mother, however, reading her book in the living room and puffing on a cigarette, seemed unaware that Holly had left.

Over the years my little sister's fits of rage became legendary. One day after school when I was winning at tennis and she had hit a particularly bad shot, she hurled her racket into the air, tore open the front of her school uniform, buttons flying every which-way, and marched off the court. Years later Holly became a very accomplished tennis player with more tempered moods, but that day she was a hornet. I stood on the court like a dolt, helpless to deal with such fury.

Perhaps the chores were a source of Holly's anger. Some days housework needed to be done, and we heard, "You children have to help me, I can't manage all this. Your brother won't do a goddamned thing, and I'm left with all the heavy work!"

Though we had maids and laundresses from time to time, a nine-bedroom house far out in the country apparently proved too much, causing them to eventually quit or, more often, just not show up for work. "That damn Nettie, she never even called," my mother sputtered.

So, between maids, Holly and I dusted bookshelves and, having heard Mom's declaration, "The doctor told me I should never vacuum," vacuumed the living room, as well. We also helped with the laundry, winding away at the old wringer washer in the basement and hoisting wet clothes up through the cellar window to the drying courtyard outside. Automatic washers and dryers were available, and my grandparents would have probably bought them for us, but our mother was a martyr to this old wringer system and refused to give it up.

In spite of our spurts of helpfulness, she was often in tears. She ran her fingers through her shock of short dark hair. "How am I supposed to take care of this house, the yard, and you children when your father never gives me any money?" Though I suspect our grandparents were supporting us, she seemed to feel impoverished. And while they sometimes sent over their lawn man to do yard work, that didn't help to assuage her distress. So Holly and I took on garden chores—clipping the crabgrass that threatened to engulf the front walkway, trimming the prickly barberry hedges—all in a futile attempt to keep our mother from her customary crying jags. "You children—" seemed to echo through the house.

Cleaning the rec room in the basement, however, was a job nobody ever got around to. This room was where we occasionally entertained friends and played ping-pong—*if* we could find a ball David hadn't dented or smashed. Below ground level, chilly and damp, the room's gritty windows looked out on the undersides of overgrown rhododendron bushes. Faulty florescent lights flickered above the ping-pong table, and the long-unswept linoleum floor was strewn with cartons of still-unpacked books from Shaker Heights. Our volumes of *The Wonderful Wizard of Oz* sat collecting mold.

The only decoration in the room was the display of ribbons Marian and Jeanie had won in horseshows. Strung along a piece of picture wire stretched across one wall of the room, the ribbons—blues, reds, yellows and whites—provided a colorful banner to accompany our games.

Later the rec room became the home of the cats. Since I'd been small I'd had a knack for attracting stray cats, and I always begged my mother to let me keep them. Soon after she gave in to my nagging, however, we discovered we had kittens in closets, kittens popping up in dresser drawers, and kittens being transported by mother cats across the living room carpet. But here at the West Hill Drive house, my mother put her foot down. She declared she detested cats; the animals would be confined to the basement.

The rapidly multiplying cats had the run of the cellar, including the laundry room, without benefit of litter boxes. Piles of cat feces soon filled every dusty corner, and driven out by the stench, we gradually lost interest in the rec room. The ping-pong table collected dust, and the elegant satin horseshow ribbons hung neglected and forgotten.

So, rather than tackle the cleaning of the rec room, Holly and I volunteered for other chores. Unfortunately, no matter how much we tried to do, my mother was still miserable. And she often refused our offers of assistance.

"Mom, can we help?" I asked one night after dinner.

"No, no, it's all right about me, children," she sighed as she scrubbed away at a crusted chili pot. A moment later we heard her wrenching cry, "I'm doing the best I can!" Later, through her sobs, after pouring herself another bourbon, she capped her plaint with, "I know you children hate me!"

"Mom, come on!" I said, beseeching her to stop. Holly and I hung our heads and wandered upstairs to our rooms.

I could have said, "We don't hate you, Mom. We love you." But those words had never become part of my vocabulary. And it would have been futile in any event. Determined to be inconsolable, she would not have heard.

But now, bumping along in my little lavender Peugeot on a sunny Friday afternoon, Holly and I head toward home with the M&M's between us. We poke our fingers into the white paper bag, bringing to our mouths the comfort of the brightly-colored chocolate morsels. We giggle at our sinful indulgence as we head for home, sharing a soothing moment. Just the two of us.

7
DAD

Sunday at noon Holly and I sat on the window seat overlooking the front lawn and driveway, waiting for our father's car to pull up. This had become our every-other-weekend ritual when we were little, a trip to Dad's house where he lived with his new wife Polly. The visits were an arrangement our parents had made, and, while I sometimes enjoyed my times with my father, I didn't always look forward to them. It seemed disloyal somehow for Holly and me to spend time with him. Plus, I felt I hardly knew him; he seemed a stranger. Nevertheless, every other Sunday we went off with Dad.

My parents had divorced when I was four; so early memories of my father are scant. He had left my mother—and us four children—for another woman. My mother's "He-ran-off-with-that-woman-and-left-me-with-you-kids" plaint had been drummed into our heads since we were old enough to listen. "That man was rotten, girls. After you were born, Jack, he told me if I got pregnant again, he'd kick my teeth in!"

My mother referred to Polly as "your father's current wife," as though there had been or would be many others. There was no escaping my mother's bitterness about this woman who had stolen her husband, leaving her stranded. But these complaints were all I knew of my father and Polly, until Holly and I started making our Sunday visits, probably when I was seven or eight.

Even by fifth grade I had little practical knowledge of my father. One day our teacher Mr. Adams went around the classroom, asking each child to name his or her father's profession. When my turn came, I wanted to climb into my desk, as I had no idea what mine did for a living. My mother had never mentioned he was an attorney in Cleveland. "I don't know," I mumbled, ashamed at my ignorance. Mr. Adams cleared his throat and moved on to the next child.

Every other Sunday at noon our father's convertible pulled up, and Holly and I ambled out the front door and clambered in. "Kisses!" he cried, offering his cheek. His two little girls placed gentle pecks on his clean-shaven face smelling of Old Spice. Off we went, with the top down in warm weather, to Tuckaway, his house in Chardon, Ohio. The scenery along Mayfield Road became more and more rural as we breezed along, small shopping centers giving way to sweeping farmland dotted with modest homes. Holly and I contributed little to a halting conversation, replying shyly to his queries about how we'd been.

"What have you been up to, Jacq?"

"Oh, . . . nothing." I replied, tongue-tied and unable to recall a single event of my week.

When I was little, my father had adopted the nickname "Jacq" for me, spelling it J-A-C-Q when he wrote me a birthday or Christmas card. The spelling made me feel special. Dad called Marian "Peanut," David "Webb," Holly "Hol," and me "Jacq." A pet name, I thought, maybe even a term of endearment. Better than "Jack," the way my mother would have spelled it. "Jack" was a boy's name, I thought, and one I hated being stuck with.

We stopped at what my father called the Old Ladies' Store to get the Sunday paper. I wandered about on the weathered floorboards of the old-fashioned general store run by two elderly sisters. The antique soda pop cooler intrigued me, and the smell of tobacco and spearmint gum saturated the air. The kindly old ladies and the warmth of the shop provided a comforting transition from Mom's house to Dad's.

During the half-hour drive, Holly and I sat in silence, the wind blowing our hair into a tangle. As we approached his address on Butternut Road, our father serenaded us in his warbly baritone, "*Ole buttermilk sky, I'm tellin' you why . . ..*" Tall and blond, sporting a yellow Izod golf shirt, he sped along in his convertible on a perfect Sunday afternoon.

Beyond a long dirt driveway lined by cow fields and meadows, we got a glimpse of the house he and Polly had recently built. The dust kicked up as we bounced along over rocky ruts, then settled as we stepped out of the car and followed a tidy brick walkway to the handsome country colonial.

And there stood Polly, a plump, pretty woman with freckles and cheery blue eyes, greeting us with a beaming smile and a hug. In spite of my mother's hateful words about her, Polly had great charm. She had taught us to knit and bake, activities that held no interest for my mother, and her house was spotless. When Holly and I occasionally spent the night at Tuckaway, our bedroom smelled of crisp linens and rose-scented soap.

The big country kitchen was clad in sunshine yellow, with pine cupboards, counters and appliances all shiny-new. The utility room off the kitchen with its modern washer and dryer smelled of bleach and fabric softener.

After Polly fixed us a lunch of egg salad sandwiches on thin-sliced white bread, my father, Holly and I played games at the wide oval cherry wood table.

"What'll it be, girls? Hangman, Gin Rummy, Blackjack, Cribbage?" He rattled off the names of all the games he'd taught us and shuffled the cards.

For the next two hours, we played and drank Cokes. At home we weren't allowed to have Coke—"It'll rot every tooth in your head!" my mother insisted. But here we could guzzle the contents of as many green-glass Coca Cola bottles as we liked, amidst cries of "Hit me!" "Twenty-one!" Blackjack!" or "Gin!"

My father was polishing his wingtips one Sunday and asked me to help. He showed me how to spread the polish with a cloth, buff the shoe with a rag, and brush the leather. Seeing my feeble attempts he ordered, "Elbow grease, Jacq, elbow grease!" and demonstrated the vigor required for the job. I grasped the brush and with all my might polished the shoes to a healthy luster. That's what elbow grease can do, I thought. Wow. Eager to show off my results and longing for praise, I lifted the heavy shoes above my head and smiled up at him. But my father had left the room.

One late winter day our father took us to a neighboring property for maple sugaring and on the walk back through the woods he taught us to spot early spring wildflowers. "Look, Jacq, there's a dog-tooth violet. Careful!" he cried, "Don't step on it!" I jumped back. A tiny plant with green-strapped leaves and brownish yellow things he said were flowers sat nestled in the melting snow. Those are flowers? I thought. Amazing. I continued along the mucky path on tiptoe, keeping a sharp eye out for other tiny plants, so I would do them no harm.

Back at the house Polly had assembled the ingredients to make brownies. "Want to help, girls?" She let us measure the bittersweet chocolate, melted butter, sugar, vanilla, and flour, stir the mixture, poor it into a pan and lick the spoon. The aroma of the baking brownies filled the room as we played cribbage. Cooled and with sifted powdered sugar on top, the moist dark chocolate cake coated our tongues and teeth and brought a guilty smile to our lips.

My father was an avid golfer, and some Sundays Holly and I found ourselves on the plush white living room carpet watching a tournament on TV. We listened to cheers and moans as Jack Nicklaus shot birdie or bogie. Our father sat on the over-stuffed chintz sofa sipping martinis, and Polly tended to her knitting. Holly and I got bored with the golf; it seemed to go on forever, and he seemed to have forgotten we were there. So we played with the sterling silver cigarette lighter on the coffee table and admired the room Polly had created—all white and pink flowery prints amidst dark wood antique tables.

From the picture window I took in the view to the fields and tree farm below. How curious to be straddling these two disparate worlds, Mom's and Dad's, I thought. It was tricky to keep my footing with no sign of a bridge between them.

When the Sunday weather was foul, instead of going out to Tuckaway, our father took us out for a hamburger and a movie. One day I begged him to take us to *Alice in Wonderland,* which was playing nearby. "Oh, no, Jacq, that's silly stuff!" he said. We went instead to a World War II flick he'd heard about, presumably so he could reminisce about his years in the Navy during the war.

I glanced longingly at boxes of Jujubes and golden popcorn as our father led us past the concession stand into the musty theatre. "Now, this is a *good* movie, girls!" We took our seats. Soon he was engrossed in the film, oblivious to Holly and me huddling in terrified silence watching ships and submarines explode across the screen and sailors drown in cold, dark seas.

When our father occasionally took us out to dinner, Holly and I had to prepare ourselves for some type of embarrassing episode, as he enjoyed devising ways to bait a hostess or waitress. It was a form of amusement for him, to discomfit her and make us laugh. One evening at an expensive restaurant at Shaker Square, Polly, Holly, and I were seated, waiting while my father parked the car. Finally he entered, and when the hostess greeted him, he pointed to our table and said, "Oh, I think I'd like to sit with those ladies!" The hostess, not realizing he was with us, suggested he sit at a table of his own. "No," he insisted, "those are pretty girls. I'd like to sit there." Flustered, the hostess followed him as he made his way towards us. "May I sit with you ladies?" he asked, a bright smile on his face. It took us only an instant to realize it was one of his pranks. "David!" Polly scolded, her way of telling him to sit down and behave. The poor hostess walked off in dismay. Holly and I sat giggling and squirming in our seats as our father, wearing a satisfied grin, settled into his chair.

While we perused our menus, he warned us not to order the Roquefort cheese dressing, as it cost extra. "You see that, girls?" he tapped his finger on the menu, "'Point five-o extra.' You don't want that." I peered up to see if he was joking. A sniff and a frown gave me the answer. But I couldn't help wondering why I wasn't worth the extra fifty cents.

When we returned from our Sunday afternoons with Dad, we often found our mother folded into a corner of the living room couch, moaning in pain, a ragged rash of welts the size of a dime running along her arms and legs—one of her hives attacks. The doctor had said they were caused by the phenobarbital she often took to settle her nerves. The term "nervous breakdown" had entered my consciousness as something she was often on the brink of, though I hardly knew what that was. In any event she sought no remedy for these hives attacks—which seemed to occur only on our Sundays with our father—but sat in agony drinking her bourbon and resisting the urge to scratch herself raw.

"Gee, Mom, what can we do?" I asked. She seemed horribly uncomfortable.

"It's all right about me, children," she said with a groan. I could tell she was irritated by my expression of concern.

Then I realized, guilt flooding my body, that we had spent a fun day with my father and Polly while my mother had been suffering here in the big house all alone. I should find some way to ease her pain, I thought. But, feeling useless, the only thing I could do was wonder. Maybe we should have stayed home.

8

AUNTIE MARIAN

The red brick house on Falmouth Road is the closest I can come to a memory of my mother's sister, Auntie Marian. When I was little, I would visit there to play with my cousin Susan. I was five and she was ten. My Auntie Marian was in the house but faceless; I do not recall ever looking into her face.

We kids played upstairs with Susan's dolls, and my cousin taught me to braid. We fashioned each other's hair into scraggly pigtails.

"Ouch!" I cried as she pulled my hairs too tight.

"Beauty has its price," she said, a phrase she must have heard from her mother.

Auntie Marian made us a lunch of broiled lamb chops with mint jelly and mashed potatoes. She always made that dish for us; maybe it was the only thing she knew how to cook.

In a damp corner of the rear yard a swing dangled from an apple tree. We played there for a while and then came inside.

One day I was put down for a nap. I lay on Auntie Marian's mahogany bed, a warm perfume-y essence arising from the bed-spread. The late afternoon sun turned the window shades a dusty amber. Outside a bird sang, repeating its haunting phrases again and again.

As I drifted off to sleep, a black swirling tunnel appeared to me. It invited me to enter. This is death, I thought. At the end of this tunnel, all is over. I was intrigued but not afraid; I knew somehow I would not be sucked into that dark place.

One day we stopped going to the red brick house on Falmouth Road. Our cousins Jeanie and Susan went to live with my grandparents for a while. Then they came to live with us on West Hill Drive.

I never asked where Auntie Marian had gone. In our family you do not pose such questions. And no explanations are offered. I knew only that my mother folded our cousins into our family, and we readily accepted them. Since my mother was a woman alone raising her own four children with some difficulty, it seemed odd. But that is what she did.

As I grew up, I overheard bits of conversation about Auntie Marian. She'd been pretty and had sung in nightclubs when she was young. She had married Uncle Doug who had a daughter named Deirdre from an earlier marriage. But then Uncle Doug got sick, and he died.

It is said Auntie Marian, at the age of thirty-seven, drank herself to death. She sat in a wing chair in her living room, staring at the portrait of her dead husband, and drank. Her shoes on the Oriental carpet made two bare spots where her feet shuffled back and forth hour after hour. One day her body, awash in grief and sherry, yielded and passed into that black tunnel.

Which is all I knew of my Auntie Marian. Until much later.

9

THE BABYSITTER

Acouple of years after we moved to West Hill Drive, my mother announced she was going to take lessons at Arthur Murray's School of Dance. "I need to lose some weight, girls." She stood in the center of the living room, winding her arms around in a curious circular motion, an exercise she must have seen on the Jack LaLanne Show. "Ballroom dancing's very good for toning up the 'figgah,' you know!" She turned her torso vigorously from side to side. "And I was quite the belle of the ball in my day."

However, in order to attend the Arthur Murray evening dance parties where she could practice her cha-cha and merengue, my mother needed a babysitter for Holly and me. The problem was finding one in rural Gates Mills.

Philip Toll was a teenager who lived in a modest brick house down the street. My mother, having given up on the sporadic help of our grandmother's gardener, had hired Philip to mow our meager lawn every week. He was a very tall boy—six feet plus—and thin. With thick glasses, a blonde crew cut, a toothy grin and a bad case of acne, he was shy and awkward.

"Girls, I've asked Philip Toll to sit with you tomorrow night."

"Philip?" What a crummy idea, I thought. "Why? I mean, maybe it would be better to have a girl babysitter," I suggested.

"Like who?" she asked, taking a sip of her sherry.

"How about Melinda who lives in that big house at the end of the street? Her mom's the one who drove us to school that first day when we missed the bus. Melinda seems nice."

When we had first moved to West Hill Drive, my mother hadn't checked the school bus schedule for our first day at Gates Mill School. Holly and I had walked in a cold drizzle up our quarter-of-a-mile driveway and along the road to the bus stop, then waited, looking to the left and right, for a bus that never came. Fortunately, Melinda and her mother were passing by on their way to school. The car stopped.

"Good morning, girls. You waiting for the bus?" Melinda's mother asked. I nodded, water dripping off my forehead.

"Oh, dear, the bus stops here at 7:45. It's 8:15 now. That bus is long gone. Want a ride?" Embarrassed by my mother's ignorance and shivering in my cotton raincoat, I'd accepted, and redheaded Melinda had offered a warm smile as we clambered into the car.

But at this moment, my mother wasn't thinking of Melinda as a babysitter candidate. "Philip is nice, too," she said. "And he probably needs the money. Besides I've already arranged it." She went back to reading her book.

On the evenings Philip sat with us, we played board games and watched TV. Holly and I didn't like our babysitter particularly, though we didn't *dis*like him; he was just a gawky guy.

Time passed slowly on West Hill Drive for a ten-year-old. When I wasn't holed up with my nose in a book, I went to my forest sanctuary or meandered about the yard, gazing up at the trees and talking to the chickadees. However, by the time I reached the age of twelve, I put all that aside and became enthralled with teen magazines and TV stars. As a result, I spent entire afternoons in reverie about who my first boyfriend might be, my first date.

I had developed a mad crush on Robert Horton, the handsome star of the "Wagon Train" TV show. Tall and well built with dark wavy hair and a tantalizing smile, he was my ideal of a first boyfriend. I fantasized about his arms around me, his face so close to mine . . .

But it was Philip Toll who first asked me out. Actually, he asked my mother for her permission, as at twelve I was rather young to be dating.

"Jack, come here a sec," my mother called as I passed by the living room. She looked up from the book she was reading. "Philip Toll wants to take you out to a movie. Saturday night. I said it was all right."

A tiny tremor ran through me. "You mean, like a date? I've never been out on a date."

"I know, but you'll start dating sooner or later." She took a draw on her cigarette and tried to find her place in the book.

"But Philip Toll? He's weird looking and . . . Do I have to? Besides, I'm too young to date, aren't I? I'm only twelve. And he's a senior in high school." My mother resumed her reading.

I had to find a way out of this. "I don't think the other girls in my class go out on dates."

"Philip Toll is a perfectly nice boy. He's only taking you out to a movie, and he's your babysitter, for heaven's sake. Besides, I feel sorry for Philip. The poor guy is so . . . gawky." She laughed. "It will boost his self-confidence if you go out with him. Plus, I've already said 'yes.'"

Oh, I thought, this is going to be really awkward. But rather than protest further, I left her to her book and wandered off to contemplate my misfortune.

The day before our date, Philip came by the house with a present for me in a plain gray cardboard box. A corsage perhaps? Peering into the box, I beheld a brand new pair of black leather shoes with 4-inch spike heels. I lifted one from the box. It was my size, 8.

"Jackie," he murmured, his eyes enlarged by his thick lenses, "would you wear these on Saturday night?"

"Uh . . . sure," I said, staring at the ghastly shoes, "I'll just check with my mother . . .." Spike heels were all the rage in the late 1950s, but for a twelve-year-old?

I offered a courteous thank you for the gift and went off to see what she would say. I found her in the kitchen making tuna and potato chip casserole.

"Mom, this is weird. Philip Toll brought me a present. He wants me to wear them on our date." I displayed the contents of the box. She glanced at the shoes and laughed.

"Mom, come on, I can't!" I cried.

"Well, what harm can it do? Don't you want to learn to wear *high heels*?" Her dark brown eyes widened in mock delight, and her dramatic delivery got me giggling. "Yes, but these are horrible!"

"Well, you'll probably wear them just this once. Think of all the trouble he went to buying them for you."

The coming event promised to be a disaster, but I decided to make my mother happy and help Philip feel good about himself. I just had to put up with a lousy first date. I went upstairs to try on the grotesque shoes.

On Saturday Philip picked me up, and we went to a movie. Crossing the lobby we must have made a colorful couple—a tall geeky guy and a page-boyed pre-teen staggering around in four-inch heels. During the film I kept praying he wouldn't put his arm around me. I was relieved when the evening was over and Philip saw me to my front door.

Polite little girl that I was, I thanked him for the evening, and as I turned the door handle to let myself into the house, he grasped my arms, leaned into me, and planted a dry, hard-lipped kiss on my mouth. It lasted only an instant, but it was a real kiss. I pulled away in horror and hurtled through the door, slamming it firmly shut.

When I was safely inside, tears of rage stung my eyes. Not only had I been caught off-guard and failed to slap his face—the way Doris Day would have done—but my first kiss, which should have been reserved for Robert Horton, had been wasted on Philip Toll. I stormed upstairs and slammed my bedroom door. Kicking off the hideous shoes, I hurled them at the wall.

"How was your date, dear?" emanated through my mother's bedroom door. I pretended not to hear, resolved to tell her nothing.

Perhaps Philip was the "perfectly nice boy" my mother saw him to be. But as I thought about it much later, he must have taken great care planning that event. He'd had to determine the difference in our heights, discover my shoe size, save his lawn mowing money for the shoes and make the purchase. He'd had to decide how he would present them to me and persuade me to wear them. And he must have spent hours dreaming of the night he would steal his first kiss.

As for me, I stashed the shoes in the back of my closet and tried to forget the whole embarrassing evening. My mother had goaded me into going out with Philip because she felt sorry for him. She perhaps considered her gesture an act of charity. But I had to wonder why his feelings were more important than mine.

And, while my mother found the situation humorous, the joke had been on me. The awkward kiss was a violation that crushed my girlish dreams, and I felt I should have been able to defend myself against it somehow. It became a secret I would carry with me for a very long time.

However, two benefits resulted from this fiasco: I graduated from needing a babysitter. And I never saw Philip Toll again.

10

ST. CHRISTOPHER'S

In my adult imagination I wander through the opening in the white picket fence and up the wide flagstone walkway, and there I am. St. Christopher's-by-the-River Episcopal Church in Gates Mills, Ohio, source of my religious education and upbringing. I revere this place and always will, though I no longer believe in anything I was taught here.

We went to church regularly when we lived in Gates Mills, not every Sunday, but most. My mother had become a member of St. Christopher's Altar Guild, the ladies who laid out the linen cloths, the flowers and Communion vessels for Sunday services. Though she grumbled about the duties, claiming she had to substitute often for other women who cancelled at the last minute, the church was likely an important social network for her, as well as a source of emotional support. So we attended services often.

St. Christopher's, set on the bank of the muddy Chagrin River, was a small parish, a petite white clapboard building with a tall steeple, a gold cross at its apex. Surrounded by a white picket fence and flanked by tall hemlock trees, it epitomized a small community church of the 1800's.

On Sunday mornings, Holly and I donned our cotton dresses and Mary Janes and went with our mother to the 9:15 service. Following her example, I knelt on a slender bench for a silent prayer before the service began. The kneeler was upholstered with coarse red carpet, and my bare knees suffered on the scratchy fibers, so I made my prayer—I didn't know exactly what I was supposed to be praying for—as short as possible.

At times the Morning Prayer service seemed interminable, especially on Communion Sundays, the first Sunday of each month. Sitting back in the pew during the Sermon or the Offertory, I basked in the eastern light beaming through the tall clear windows. The crimson aisle carpet and the white wooden pews provided perfect order. The aromas of incense and floor polish blended with the heady fragrance of the ladies' Chanel No. 5, and the steps of latecomers creaked on the antique polished floorboards at the back. During lengthy sermons I struggled to focus on the words of the handsome, silver-haired Dr. Pattie, but my eyes wandered to the simple effects before me—a white wall, a lectern, a flag, an altar adorned by a pressed linen cloth, seasonal flowers, and a sturdy gold cross. My gaze took in the backs of the women parishioners in their pastel veiled hats and their husbands in gray suits and starched white collars.

Kneeling beside my mother during the Prayer of Confession, I turned my head to peek at her as she prayed. Her head bowed, her eyes closed, her hands folded and supporting her forehead, she was absorbed in the act of prayer. What was she praying about? I wondered. Did she have sins that needed confessing? It seemed unlikely.

Mimicking her, I bowed my head, resting my forehead on the backs of my folded hands and muttered along with the congregation,

> "... *and there is no health in us. But thou, O*
> *Lord, have mercy upon us, miserable offenders.*
> *Spare thou those, O God, who confess their faults.*
> *Restore thou those who are penitent ...*"

Though I was uncertain of what sins I had committed, the repetition of these words week after week became ingrained in my consciousness. A loving, forgiving God was watching over me. As long as I lived a righteous life, following my mother's example, I would be rewarded.

My mother attempted to instill basic Christian principles into our daily lives. When, as a twelve-year-old suffering the angst of being shy and unpopular, I went to ask her advice.

"Mom, nobody likes me!" I laid my head on the kitchen table and sobbed. My peers seemed to avoid me, maybe because of my scraggly brown hair or my occasional acne, or maybe it was my rear end that burst through the seams of my summer cotton shorts. I couldn't figure out how to fix these inadequacies.

"Stop thinking about yourself, dear," my mother said. "Think of others and their needs, and you won't have time to worry about your own problems." It seemed a solid Christian doctrine to live by. So I resolved to follow her suggestion with the hope that my insecurities—and my big rear end—would vanish.

By the age of thirteen, I had become an ardent believer in a merciful God who took care of me and provided me with many blessings. Contrite, respectful and devout, I knelt each night on the hardwood floor at the side of my little white canopy bed and prayed. I knew it was wrong to pray for things—like a new polo coat or a record player. Taking my cue from the movie *The Nun's*

Story, I prayed to find a way to be a good Christian, helpful to others, a faithful, obedient member of the church. And I prayed for my mother, that she might be relieved of her anxious moods and somehow be made happy.

My little white leather-bound prayer book, *The Book of Common Prayer*, sat on my bedside table, close at hand. My godfather, Father Peterson, the priest at my grandmother's church had given it to me. With its soft pebbly cover and a slim gold satin ribbon to hold the place for a favorite prayer, I saw it as the talisman that would keep me grounded in faith.

My piety was short-lived, however, as my teenage years took hold. Instead of praying solo at the side of my bed, I joined the church Youth Group. On Sundays we celebrated the Evening Prayer service together and went away on weekend retreats. I also sang each morning in the adult choir. The church, a safe warm nest, a source of friends and music making, became my buffer from adolescent angst.

But there was a price to be paid to become a true member of the Episcopal Church—learning the Catechism. For Confirmation Sunday, a ceremony where thirteen-and fourteen-year olds were inducted into the Church by the Bishop of the Diocese, we were required to memorize the Creed and the entire Catechism, an unending list of questions and answers affirming the tenets of the Church. The Bishop would be calling on those to be confirmed at random, asking us one of the many questions and expecting the perfect recitation of a response. I'd never met the Bishop, but I feared he might be a cranky sort, and that to flub a response to one of his questions would result in severe chastisement and shame.

The Catechism could be learned only by rote, as the archaic language was incomprehensible. I loved the church, but struggling to grasp the meaning of the text of this rite was beyond me. My mother helped me study; we went over the questions and answers again and again.

"How many parts are there in this Sacrament?" she read from the prayer book.

"Two, the outward visible sign, and the inward spiritual grace."

"What is the outward visible sign or form in Baptism?"

"Water; wherein the person is baptized . . . uh . . ."

The rest of the response was a blank. My mother cued me, and I stuttered the proper answer.

"What is the inward and spiritual grace?"

"A death unto sin, and a new birth . . . unto righteousness; for being by nature born in sin, and . . ." —my brain was churning— " . . . the children of wrath, we are hereby made the children of grace."

"What is required of persons to be baptized?"

"Uh . . . " Blank. "I give up. I don't *know*. Mom, I don't understand what any of this means! Why do I have to do this?" I whined.

"Because I said so," she declared. So there was no way out. Confirmation was that coming Sunday, the entire catechism had to be memorized word for archaic word, and that was that.

On Confirmation Sunday the Bishop did call on me. With drippy palms I rose from the pew and bumbled through some feebly recalled response he seemed to accept. When I finished, I sank into my seat feeling I'd escaped with my life. Such was my induction to full-fledged membership in the Episcopal Church.

Had I stayed at home with my mother and continued at St. Christopher's, I might have remained a faithful member of the church. But I went away to college. The school I chose was a small Methodist university in Indiana where my primary interest was theatre. My freshman year I studied philosophy, thinking it might provide me background on the development of religious beliefs. I also enrolled in biology to explore the mysteries of natural science.

On Sundays I occasionally attended the Methodist Church, but without the attendant rituals of the Episcopal service I'd come to revere, the place felt empty. The towering stone sanctuary lacked the intimacy of St. Christopher's. And the words of the service seemed simplistic and prosaic; they no longer made sense to me. Nor, I realized in the months to follow, did the concept of God.

I was learning in Philosophy101 how the early great thinkers struggled with the idea of the existence of God. If even Aristotle and Plato had to wrestle with the concept of a Supreme Being, I came to ponder, maybe there was no such thing. Perhaps God was a myth invented by man to placate his fear of the unknown—and nothing more.

Then one clear Sunday morning, I had an epiphany. Sitting in the vaulted stone space listening to a simple-minded sermon extolling the beauty of Nature as a gift from God, I was struck: this is absurd. Nature is its own creation, not God's; it evolved, as did the Universe. What has God to do with it? And where is the proof, I mused further, that He even exists?

In time my youthful mind came to a stunning conclusion: there is no God. There was no Supreme Being, no loving Father, looking over us, hearing our prayers, I decided. If there were, why were young soldiers and innocent people being blown up in Vietnam? And why did pain and suffering persist despite the ardent prayers of millions? There was no rational answer. The whole concept of a merciful deity was a curious sham, I concluded. Worshipping God, confessing sins and sipping wine from a chalice were without meaning. There was no God.

After years of careful thought on this matter, I resolved not to return to church. But, fearing she'd be disheartened, I never shared my newfound disbelief with my mother.

Over the years, my love of music has necessitated a connection to the church. A singer since childhood, I was encouraged by my mother, who started me on voice lessons at age thirteen. Since then, I've sung in choirs, glee clubs, and chorales, often as a soloist or section leader. Privileged to sing the great works of Bach, Brahms, and Mozart, I have always been thrilled by their soaring melodies and exalted texts. But for years, rather than singing in Sunday services at which I'd feel compelled to feign prayer, I performed in groups offering afternoon or evening concerts where I wouldn't have to suffer through a liturgy.

When on occasion my choral group would participate in an Ash Wednesday service, I made a sincere effort to hear the words of the service. However, straining to absorb scripture, prayers, creed and hymns, I came up empty. I remained unconvinced there was a supreme being. Beyond honoring the powerful teachings of Jesus, his instruction in compassion and brotherly love, I was at an impasse when it came to embracing a belief in God. The little white prayer book I had revered as a child no longer had relevance.

As I got into my fifties, my singing abilities and opportunities diminished, but I was unwilling to give up music. My mother had instructed me never to abandon my "God-given" talent, and I longed to express myself with my voice as long as I possibly could. So I decided I'd put my principles aside and join an Episcopal Church choir; I was willing to endure Sunday services in order to continue performing.

After singing for Michael the choirmaster, I was accepted. Then I checked the fit of the choir robe he'd assigned me. I glanced in the mirror, and was confronted by the dismal image of an aging over-grown acolyte. Oh, I thought, I've just made a *huge* mistake. This isn't me at all. But by then I'd agreed to join the choir. There was no way out. I'd just have to fake it.

From the next room Michael, fishing to see if I would be familiar with the service in which I'd be singing, asked me, "So, I was wondering, did you grow up in any particular denomination?"

"Episcopal, actually," I replied, trying to sound breezy, knowing it had been thirty-five years since I'd willingly attended an Episcopal service.

On my first Sunday as a choir member, the familiar fragrances of incense and floor polish took me right back to St. Christopher's. Though nervous about my new role, I felt at home in the sanctuary, that somehow belonged. Perhaps I can go back, I thought, as I sat in the chancel listening to the familiar words of the prayers. Back to the days when I believed.

Over the next months as I became accustomed to the service again—it had been modernized from the one I'd known as a child—I sensed the wrongness of my presence in that place. Sitting behind the Communion table, facing the congregation, I muttered all the prayers, sang the many anthems and hymns, and recited the Creed, but I still couldn't reconcile the nonsensical words. I kept coming back to my true conviction: for me the idea of God the Father is absurd.

In time, uttering words I did not believe, service after service—the prayer book clenched in my steaming palms—became intolerable. One morning as we sang an anthem based on the Twenty-third Psalm, my throat tightened, and I choked on the words. My blue choir robe hung on me, the cloak of a hypocrite. You liar, I thought, you fraud. And so, after almost five years of agonizing over whether or not I could bear to give up singing and analyzing other reasons I was unhappy in the church, I quit the choir and relieved myself of a troublesome burden.

I still attend church services occasionally. I sit in the sanctuary to contemplate my life's design and to re-hear the stories of Christ's teachings. But I do not believe in God. All mention of "His" words or deeds rankles my rational self.

And yet, something about the church puzzles me. Why, in spite of my disbelief, does my heart lift as I listen to an Evensong service? Why do my eyes tear as I sing the ancient hymns of Easter and Christmas? And why do I maintain an odd sense of pleasure in being a member of the Episcopal Church? While I abjure the doctrine of the church, it seems I cannot completely divorce myself from it. Holding the dogma at arm's length, I cling, perhaps, to the comfort of ritual and a sense of community the church provides. And to the memories of my mother kneeling in St. Christopher's, muttering to her God the Prayer of Confession.

My little white leather-bound *Book of Common Prayer*, however, has gone missing—literally. I've searched all the bookshelves, drawers, and cupboards in the house. It is nowhere to be found. But where did it go? How does one dispose of a prayer book? Take it to Goodwill? Donate it to the library book sale? Toss it in the trash bin with the banana peels and damp paper towels?

I don't know how it came to be missing. But it is gone. I'm sure of that. I've looked.

11

THE LITANY

Holly and I, about twelve and fourteen, sat at the candlelit dinner table and listened again as my mother described her tortured childhood.

"When I was a child, my parents hid me away in a closet when company came," she told us.

"Oh, come on, Mom," I protested, stirring the mashed potatoes on my plate. We'd heard it so many times before.

"No, they did!" Her sharp tone made me wince. "They hid me away because I was so ugly!"

Inwardly I scoffed at this remark. Our grandparents, pillars of Cleveland society, had probably been of the children-are-to-be-seen-and-not-heard school, but I doubted they had ever shut a little girl in a closet.

And my mother was not ugly, though she seemed to think she was. She had scars around her jaw, and her teeth were unevenly spaced, as though they had been forced apart somehow, but she was tall and slender with short, dark wavy hair swept up off her face.

She had high cheekbones and wide nostrils. I considered her looks distinctive; she was not ugly to me.

"All I ever heard about," she went on, "was your Auntie Marian, how *perfectly lovely* she was and Uncle Dick, how he was such a *fine* tennis player." My mother, a glass of bourbon close at hand, had difficulty lifting her dinner fork to her mouth. She leaned forward, stretching her tongue over an excessively dropped jaw, and brought the food to it, the forkful nearly toppling onto her plate. She looked sleepy, and her body threatened to careen into her plate.

She was exhausted raising us all by herself, that I knew. "Your father ran off with that woman and left me alone with you children. And, you know, he's never once helped to pay for your education . . ." She launched into another familiar tirade.

My mother chewed her food and swallowed. "How's your schoolwork coming, girls?" Holly and I gave cursory responses. "OK, I guess." "Fine."

We knew that at Laurel School for Girls, an exclusive private school in Shaker Heights, my mother had gotten straight A's in all her studies when she was a girl. She had been obliged to, as Laurel had made an odd arrangement whereby another student's scholarship to the school had depended on my mother's excellent performance.

"That girl wouldn't have been able to go to *school* if I hadn't made perfect marks! I *had* to do it. I worked like a *dog* at that school." She took a quaff of her bourbon.

Holly and I stared at our plates. I was unsure how to respond, as I'd heard the story so often. I felt fortunate to be going to Laurel School—especially since my father didn't pay for it—but I knew my efforts there could never measure up to my mother's.

"I had perfect marks," she reminded us, "and I was president of my class. But Uncle Dick and Auntie Marian got all the praise—*he* was so athletic, *she* was so beautiful. And, you know what? My parents never once told me 'Good for you.'" She tilted her bourbon glass where little remained but slivers of ice.

She sighed. "You'll never be Number One girls, never. You may be good at your studies or at singing or at playing tennis, but you'll never be on top. You'll never be Number One."

Whether my mother was expressing her own regret, or preparing us for life's disappointments, I do not know. But what I heard each time she repeated that phrase was that *I* would never be Number One, ever, in anybody's eyes.

I twitched in my seat, hoping to hear a break in the litany so I could excuse myself from the table.

"Can you imagine that, girls? They never said 'Good for you.' Not once!" She pierced a slice of rare roast beef and sawed at it with her knife.

I wanted to make my mom feel better. Maybe I should have said "Good for you" right then, to allay her sorrowful mood, but the words would not surface to my lips.

"Can I be excused?" I rose from the table, the feet of my chair scraping on the bare hardwood floor. "I have a lot of homework."

"Not once," she said, lost in long ago.

12

MAMAMA'S

"Come on, kids! Let's get going!" our mother called up to us. "We have to be at Mamama's by one o'clock!"

My mother never needed to call us more than once for a trip to Mamama's. Every other Sunday—the ones when Holly and I didn't go off with Dad—we went for a formal luncheon at our grandmother's. And every hot summer afternoon we swam in her splendid silver pool. A world apart from Bleak House, Mamama's was a haven we always looked forward to.

Our grandmother was called Mamama, because my sister Marian, the first grandchild, had uttered these infantile syllables as she gazed into her grandmother's pale blue eyes. The name suited the elegant reserved woman we came to view with affection.

Our grandfather was called Baba. When I was little, I enjoyed rides on the cloth upholstery of his cream-colored Packard and the popcorn he popped for us. A prominent Cleveland attorney, he was portrayed in photographs as a quiet, dignified man who often smoked a pipe or cigar. Baba died of oral cancer when I was small, and I lost the chance to get to know him.

Warm thoughts of my grandmother fill my head: Mamama sitting in her favorite chair in her library, Mamama serving up a plum pudding for Christmas dinner, and Mamama tottering out to the pool to see if her grandchildren were having fun. A small, handsome woman with grey hair gathered up with combs and a fine white hairnet, she was raised in an aristocratic Boston family, and her primary activity seemed to be keeping her family and servants in line. She always wore a silk print dress and block-heeled shoes, and her delicate voice had a distinct upper-crust lilt. She often walked from room to room whistling—a thin wavery, nearly tuneless stream of air passing through her pursed lips. Mamama's demeanor toward us seemed to stop just short of tenderness, yet we were very fond of her.

My grandparents had built their house in Lyndhurst, Ohio, during the early thirties. A large home, though not ostentatious, it sprawled in different directions, offering an assortment of intriguing rooms to explore. The two-story structure was fashioned with sturdy blocks of gray and brown sandstone adorned by a black roof and wood trim. Surrounded by wide lawns, lilac and perennial gardens, and fruit trees, the house nestled comfortably into the landscape.

In the front hall, the smell of antique wood and Old English furniture polish permeated the air. The first thing we kids did when we arrived—after hanging up coats, storing boots, and admiring ourselves in the full-length mirror in the cloak room—was to dig our hands into the "gum hole." Sitting on a limestone shelf in the front hall, the old humidor held a stash of Blackjack and Teaberry chewing gum and packets of SenSen, tiny anise-flavored pellets that melted onto our tongues. As many times as we reached into the gum hole, we were never disappointed; treats were always there.

After raiding the gum hole, we greeted Mamama in the library, her center of operations. While she and my mother sipped cocktails and compared notes on who in the community had married, died, or was in or out of the Social Register, I sat on the sturdy leather fender in front of the fireplace and pondered the contents of the floor-to-ceiling dark oak bookcases framing the windows. In winter, there was always a fiery blaze to warm me.

In summer, I slid back and forth on the black leather seat seeking my mother's attention while eavesdropping and observing. She seemed relaxed on these afternoons, engaged in conversation with her mother, perhaps feeling temporarily relieved of the responsibilities of a big home and six children.

After Steve the butler served tomato—pronounced by Mamama "tomahto"—juice garnished with lemon slices, we moved to the dining room for our formal Sunday lunch. On these occasions we wore our best clothes, clean white blouses and plaid kilt skirts, and exhibited impeccable manners. The mahogany table gleamed beneath a lace tablecloth laid with delicate china, glistening sterling silver and crystal. Mamama carved a standing rib roast and passed us each a slice. Steve went from one person to another serving us vegetables and roasted potatoes.

The most intriguing object in the dining room was the buzzer. After we'd eaten our meal, while waiting for our dessert of ice cream and cake, one of us would pipe up, "Mamama, can we try the buzzer?" Discretely hidden beneath the carpet near the head of the table was a round brass buzzer Mamama pressed with her foot to call the butler when something was needed from the kitchen or dishes were to be cleared. We found this a most amazing gadget and would take turns pressing it to see what would happen. We climbed under the table, pressed the buzzer, heard a raspy hum off in the kitchen, and waited to see if we could get Steve to come out. He always appeared on demand but, after several repetitions of our prank, a scowl clouded his face.

"That's enough, children," Mamama said. We scurried back to our chairs.

Sometimes after lunch I would wander into the living room and sit down at the baby grand piano to muddle through the one Haydn sonatina I'd memorized or perhaps the first sixteen measures of the "Moonlight Sonata." Soon disgusted with my incompetent playing, I threw myself onto the overstuffed couch by the fireplace. The fragrance of the Oriental carpet and the lingering aroma of burnt logs enveloped me. Oil portraits of Scottish ancestors lined the walls. Dark oak beams criss-crossed the high plaster ceiling. I stared at them and pondered what I might do to fill a wintry afternoon.

Some days Steve set up the 8-millimeter projector to show home movies. We never tired of watching the movies Mamama had taken of us playing outside—dancing about and making silly faces at the camera. The film captured the annual Memorial Day picnic with Steve serving cocktails from a linen-covered tray and barbequing lamb chops amidst clouds of smoke. Jerky moving pictures of Mamama's prized daffodil field and peony garden, babies staggering on the lawn, children and adults playing croquet, toddlers climbing up and rolling down a grassy slope, and boys diving and cannonballing into the pool entertained us for hours. As soon as we discovered we could run these movies backwards, we made ourselves sick with laughter and screamed at whoever was at the projector, "Play it again! Play it again!"

Christmas at Mamama's was bedlam, with my siblings and me, Jeanie and Susan, and our six cousins on the other side of the family, the Inglises, all tearing at packages that had been piled around the tree. The girls untied satin ribbons to discover gifts of handkerchiefs and polo coats, while the boys got puzzles and games they refused to share with the girls. Over the din we all shouted polite thank you's to Mamama.

Mamama and Baba always had a couple working for them as butler/chauffeur and cook/laundress, and the pair we came to know best was Steve and Barbara. Steve, with his thick Eastern European accent and stern expression, frightened me a bit. But his wife Barbara, a stout, grey-haired lady we never saw outside the kitchen, had a kindly smile and an ample supply of sugar cookies she'd bake for us. During frequent trips to the kitchen we each helped ourselves to a bottle of ginger ale from the refrigerator, said a bashful hello and thank you to Barbara, gathered as many cookies as we could grasp in one hand, and made our way out through the butler's pantry to wherever we were playing.

I was fascinated by the butler's pantry and often lingered there, if Steve and Barbara were not nearby. Behind the leaded-glass windows of the cupboards sat handsome cobalt blue goblets and leaded crystal stemware evoking images of elegant parties of an earlier era. Nibbling a cookie, I walked through the dining room to survey the glass display case in a passageway to the front hall. Precious objects my grandparents had inherited or acquired on their travels lined the glass shelves, among them miniature portraits, antique sherry glasses, and an exotic ivory fan from some distant time and place.

Occasionally Mamama would allow us into her secret safe. She would remove a certain book from a certain library shelf, press a hidden button, and the bookshelf would click and swing away from the wall. Within was a tiny room that held boxes full of jewelry and sterling silver pieces Mamama prized. One by one she would name each treasure and let us hold it and imagine how it might be worn or used for a formal occasion.

After one of Mamama's annual trips to Bermuda she brought back a game called Skittles, a British game similar to billiards but played on a smaller table. She had become proficient at it, and on summer days she urged us to join her on the sun porch to play. The object of the game was to cue a ball into any of six holes without knocking over little wooden skittles, like miniature bowling pins, protecting them. Holly, Susan, and I played with her for hours. Our aristocratic grandmother edging around the table with a cue stick in her hands was a sight to behold.

A lot of Mamama-isms remain with us, remarks such as "If I eat any more, I shall die in the night!" or "Slimming today?" when one of us failed to finish our meal. When a new grandchild joined the family, her quaint expression of affection was, "Oh, isn't he cunning?" We laughed at her love of Geraci's pizza, her inability to see over the steering wheel when she drove, and her habit of sniffing to show disapproval of someone's actions.

One day while walking along Euclid Avenue in downtown Cleveland—Mamama was treating Holly and me to lunch at the Union Club—she halted on the sidewalk and looked down at her feet. There sat her baggy silk underpants, which had apparently lost their elastic. Without missing a beat, Mamama stepped out of her drawers, bent down to retrieve them, tucked them into her handbag, and continued down the city sidewalk. "Come along, girls," she said.

After one Sunday lunch I slipped away unnoticed and went upstairs to explore the intriguing sights and sounds there. I adored Mamama's bedroom with its intense fragrances of lavender soap and face powder. I ran my fingers over the blown glass perfume bottles on her dressing table, tinkered with the handsome scissor and letter opener set on her antique writing desk, and stretched out on the chaise longue where she took her late afternoon nap.

Nearby was Baba's bedroom; I stepped in to investigate his collection of leather-bound books. Sitting in my grandfather's rocking chair by the window, I pulled a random volume from the shelf, and tried to make sense of it. The prose was unintelligible, yet I allowed myself the fantasy of being able to fathom the books Baba himself had read.

I walked along the dark angled corridor, trailing my fingertips along the coarse painted stucco wall, and stopped at the Rose Room. Here I played Mamama's collection of glass-topped music boxes, the delicate picks on the cylinders plucking the iron pins, the sound transporting me to faraway places. I lay down on the chenille bedspread and fondled the old-fashioned stuffed animals I imagined to have been my mother's. I wondered if this had been her room when she was a teenager.

On rare occasions, Holly and I spent the night at Mamama's. After dinner we climbed up onto the high four-poster beds in the Green Room and folded ourselves into tightly tucked starched white sheets. "Good night, girls," Mamama said and turned out the light. "Let me know if you need anything." She closed the door, and we heard her block heels toddling down the hall. And then, wrapped in the safety and security of absolute quiet, we fell asleep.

On summer afternoons the main attraction at Mamama's was the long concrete swimming pool with its silver-painted walls. Hours upon hours were spent with cousins of all ages racing laps, splashing each other, jumping, and diving from the high stone platform at the deep end. Shouts of "Mom, Mom! Look at this!" "Watch this, Mom!" "Mom, look what I can do!" flew through the air. But my mother, engaged in witty repartee with Mamama's neighbor, Mrs. Weir, was deaf to our cries.

After a swim Holly and I lay on the hot flagstone path at the edge of the pool to warm up and dry off. The steaming stone smelled of minerals and desiccated bird droppings. Resting my wet head on my folded arms, I observed my family. Marian, Jeanie, and Susan sunned themselves in woven plastic lounge chairs, rubbing their limbs with baby oil. They basked in the brilliant light of record album covers lined with tin foil, competing for the best tan. My mother's skin, however, was always the darkest, nearly mahogany. Mamama chose to sit in the shade nearby, cool in her flowered silk dress, to watch her grandchildren have a fine time.

After swimming we ran around the concrete tennis court with our wooden rackets and white Dunlop tennis balls. Or we played whiffle ball on the wide lawn full of clover, side-stepping hundreds of honeybees drunk with nectar. Or we wandered through the orchard, inspecting the cherry and apple trees for signs of early fruit.

Our mother instructed us at the end of each day at our grandmother's to say, "Thank you, Mamama, for a very nice time," which we did. Later that "thank you" became extended as we drove away down the long driveway, laughing and yelling at the top of voices, "THANK YOU FOR A VERY VERY VERY VERY VERY NICE TIME!!!"

Mamama died when I was sixteen. A few days before her death I went to visit her. As a result of an unsuccessful cataract surgery, she had lost her right eye. Other complications had brought her close to death, and she was now at home under nurses' care. An antiseptic steel hospital bed had been wheeled into her elegant blue bedroom.

"Hi, Mamama!" I said, trying to sound cheerful. "How are you feeling?"

I winced at her appearance. My proud, dignified grandmother, always so upright and solid, was now a helpless lump on the bed, with a white gauze bandage where her right eye had been. Her left eye was fixed in a fierce stare, her teeth clenched in a horrifying grimace. Perhaps in too much pain to speak, Mamama was motionless. While her pale dry lips were silent, her eye seemed to scream with anguish, as though begging, "Stop! Make the agony stop!"

I stood paralyzed wanting to ask the nurse, "Can't you do something for her? She's in pain!" but I was too shy. A hot wind rushed through my heart. Perhaps Mamama's intense stare was imploring "Leave, leave me—now!" Feeling an intruder—my grandmother would never have wanted to be seen in this condition—I retreated and left the house without actually saying goodbye.

After Mamama died, many of her fine possessions were divided between my mother and Uncle Dick, and others put up for sale. Soon the beloved house was sold. Pained to see it go, we kept in touch with the new owners and requested occasional visits. But at those times I was shocked by the changes I saw. The dark oak beams in the living room ceiling had been painted white, and the gorgeous pool, now enclosed by a chain link fence, had been ruined by the addition of a plastic aquamarine slide.

The property went through one or two more owners. Finally, it landed in the hands of a developer who bulldozed the house, the lawn, the gardens, the pool, and the tennis court, to build a shopping center and parking lot. He called the development "Legacy Village."

I was heartsick, as were my siblings and Jeanie and Susan. That property had surely been *our* legacy. What a tragedy that my mother and Uncle Dick had let the house and gardens slip away to be demolished.

When Mamama died, Father Peterson said, "With her goes the end of an era." He was right; hers was a lifestyle that, at least for the members of our family, would never be experienced again. All that remains to us from that house are several oil paintings, random pieces of antique furniture, and a few curled photos. But for these, each and every one, I am so grateful.

The home movies, now DVD's, of our silly showing-off for Mamama's camera remain, as well. I watch those movies today with a sense of wonderment rather than delight, astonished that my childhood should have encompassed such privilege and pleasure.

Thank you, Mamama, for a very, very, VERY nice time.

13

JIGSAW PUZZLE

After Marian and Jeanie each married and set up their own households, and David and Susan were spending most of the year at college, my mother apparently decided she'd had enough of trying to keep up the big colonial on West Hill Drive, so we moved. We left behind the ravines, the bunkhouse, and the long gravel driveway and relocated to nearby Chesterland where she had bought a modest, hopefully more manageable, house.

Set back in a woodsy rural lot, our new home, an unglamorous split-level with five bedrooms, was divided into three levels with two distinct living areas, upper and lower. Why she thought such an arrangement suited our family was unclear, but perhaps she felt the separate spaces would allow her more solitude.

With the onset of the first winter, it was obvious the steep drive-way was going to be a problem. After the first big snowstorm the snowplow hadn't arrived and we needed to get to school (Laurel School rarely closed for a snow day), so my mother decided we'd have to forge our way up the drive through the two-foot drifts, with-out the benefit of snow tires. I crossed my fingers as she headed the car through a sea of white. We plowed along the level part of the drive, fishtailing from side to side. Then she gunned it to ascend the steep slope to the road. The wheels spun. She gunned it again, again and again; we were slipping and sliding and going nowhere.

"Girls, get out and push. I'll try again." Holly and I hopped out, waded through thigh-high snow, and leaned our weight against the rear taillights, but the tires kept spinning. Soon the smell of burnt rubber pierced the cold. As my mother put it in reverse to try to get some traction, the car rolled backward and slid off the drive into a drift.

"We'll have to dig it out, girls," she said. I trudged off to get a shovel, but no amount of digging with a garden spade—the snow shovel had been irretrievably lost somewhere on the property—could release the tires from the heavy white snow. We were stuck at home till a tow truck could come to haul the car out and set us free.

We plodded back to the house to warm ourselves with hot chocolate, if any could be found. Ill at ease with the unaccustomed free time, I wandered around the house. I'd rather be in school, I thought, doing something productive. The emptiness of the day began to wear. "There's nothing to *do*," I whined at my mother. "What's there to *do*?"

Seated on the blue living room sofa trying to read, my mother lifted her gaze to acknowledge my complaints. "Then *find* something to do!" she said, "Watch television. Go read a good book!"

Holly and I had tried watching TV, of course. But on a snowy day like this, it entailed more effort than it was worth. First, I had to find the set of pliers. Stowed away in a downstairs kitchen drawer under rolls of wax paper, burnt out light bulbs, and books of Green Stamps, the pliers were used to turn on the TV set, as the on/off knob had been broken and lost many months ago. After getting the set turned on, I jiggled the antenna on top, angling it towards Cleveland some thirty miles away, to get decent reception. The screen blipped with vibrating stripes. I fiddled with the horizontal hold on the back of the set, Holly monitoring from the front, until at last we had a viewable picture. But in five minutes the screen went to snow again, and deciding there was nothing good on anyway— just some stupid soap opera—we gave up.

In the upstairs hall and the downstairs living room there were built-in bookshelves loaded with books we could have pulled off the shelf. But the dusty hardbacks my mother had read had no appeal. There was a complete set of Encyclopedia Britannica we might have leafed through, but we weren't even tempted to take one from its place. Not only were the contents unfathomable, with tiny black and white line drawings posing as illustrations, but the books were wedged into the shelf so tight, and stuck together so tightly with mold and mildew, that pulling out volume "G-J," for example, would be an arduous task and jamming it back into place impossible.

From my slouched position in a wing chair nearby, I studied my mother. Her calm gaze at the page before her belied the loneliness I had perceived at other times. Her fixed stare into the back yard had often revealed a deep longing I imagined could never be satisfied. A woman living under the stigma of divorce, her older children off on their own and few friends to offer distraction, she was left with only her two younger girls for company. Two annoying girls now intent on dragging her from her book.

Our anxious presence disturbed her. Slapping the book onto the sofa cushion beside her, she looked up and said, "Well, why don't you girls do a puzzle? I think there's one in the cupboard downstairs."

"Oh, yeah, OK!" So Holly and I galumphed down to the lower living room to fetch the jigsaw puzzle. There was always a puzzle that our mother had given us for Christmas and had been stashed away for a snowy day. We searched through various drawers and shelves and finally found one amidst musty photo albums and tangled strings of Christmas lights in a cupboard by the fireplace.

I thought about taking a moment to straighten out the Christmas lights, but put the thought aside. Hastily pulled from this past year's tree, bunched up and stuffed into the cupboard, they were in a hopeless snarl, some bulbs missing, others broken. It would take ages to clear that dusty intertwined mass, so I jammed them back onto the shelf and shut the door.

That Christmas had been chaos, as usual. Our mother had bought the tree, wrested it into the house, and struggled to set it up by herself.

"Can we help you, Mom?" Why did she have to do everything herself?

"No, no, it's all right, dear, I'll just . . . " She knelt and, holding the seven-foot tree with one arm, tried to steady it in the stand. The tree listed to one side and toppled directly onto her.

"Mom!" Holly and I rushed to rescue her. Finally, after working together to pull the tree upright and stabilize it in the stand, we started sorting through ornaments, untangling silver tinsel, and decorating.

Shopping and wrapping presents presented a daunting task for my mother each year. On one Christmas Eve, while Holly and I sat watching an Andy Williams TV special, she took a swig from her drink, knelt on the floor in front of us, and wrestled in the dim lamplight with piles of oversized boxes, rolls of wrapping paper and ribbon, scissors, and tape.

"I'll never get these presents wrapped in time!" she cried. "We have to be at the midnight service in an hour!" Exhausted, she worked herself into a frenzy, tearing at bits of paper that wouldn't fold, ripping streams of tape from the dispenser, losing track of the scissors and scrabbling around to find them. She was near tears, and I wondered if I should be helping her wrap my own presents.

We knew she had tons of presents for us stashed in her closet. Games and toys and clothes and shoes and silly hats we never wore and nightgowns and bedroom slippers and gadgets for which there were no batteries and never would be. Her gifts, sometimes practical, often whimsical, were the source of oohs and ahs and thank yous and screams of laughter every Christmas morning. Even though I loved getting presents, this embarrassment of riches made me uncomfortable; it made us beholden to her somehow, and I wondered why she felt she had to buy us so much.

But her reaction to the gifts I gave her always pleased me. "Ooooh! I've never heard of such a thing!" she'd say with a laugh, lifting a striped flannel nightgown from the gift box I'd presented her. "Never *heard* of such a thing!"

But on this day when we were snowbound, I pulled the jigsaw puzzle from the cupboard and tore off the cellophane wrapper while Holly set up the card table. The teal blue imitation leather-topped table with a cigarette burn near one corner had seen better days. One of the folding metal legs was damaged and splayed out, but the table was sturdy enough, as long as nobody leaned on it. Doing so would cause the product of hours of puzzle solving to cascade to the floor.

A chill pervaded the lower living room, and we could never get the thermostat to work, so Holly and I moved the card table near the fireplace. I found a few pieces of dry firewood scattered around the garage floor, and, once I'd yanked at the stubborn metal screen and laid some logs, I got a modest fire going. Soon we were settled in to our puzzle.

We studied the image of a country cottage, flower garden, and rippling stream, then, sifting through pieces in the box, analyzed each one, and fit the bits together till the border, then the interior images, took shape. The surrounding silence was punctuated only by, "That's not right! That can't go there!" and "Yes, it can. Look, perfect fit!"

As we got deep into our puzzle, the thought of my mother upstairs all by herself started to nag at me. It seemed a shame to be enjoying this activity without her. Maybe she was lonely. Should I stop what I was doing and go up to keep her company? Or did she prefer to be alone? Undecided, I dropped the thought and continued our project.

Before long, Holly got bored with the puzzle and wandered off. I was pleased to be left alone, engrossed with bits of color and texture that engaged with others just so. The sense of accomplishment derived from fitting myriad fragments into a unified idyllic scene was tremendously gratifying.

Near the end of the day, my mother came downstairs to join me. She stabbed at the smoldering fire with a brass poker, and, switching on a floor lamp, hovered over the card table with her glass of bourbon.

"Need some help?" she asked.

"Sure." I looked up at her. "Be careful, though, don't lean on the table."

She pulled up a chair. Her strong weathered fingers with unvarnished nails combed through the puzzle box. Pulling out pieces I never would have chosen to add to the mix, she tried to fit something into what I'd already laid out.

"There, there's a good one!" she exclaimed as she forced two pieces together that were clearly not a match. She took a sip of her drink with a satisfied smile. I didn't bother to correct her mistake; I'd fix it later. Rather, I sat by her side and drew in the fragrance of her cigarette smoke and the warm aroma of bourbon on her breath. She was offering me her help, imperfect and unsteady as it was, and I was accepting it. We continued on in silence, bent over our shared task, fitting the pieces, making it work.

Roars of an engine and clanking of chains outside broke the spell of our tranquil moment. We ran upstairs to the front window to watch the flashing lights of the tow truck as it maneuvered back and forth through the snow, pulling our car from the drift and parking it safely on the road.

14

UNCLE MINKIE

The following spring my mother had the Chesterland house painted a cheery yellow. Without the albatross of the huge West Hill Drive house around our necks, we seemed on our way to a calmer, simpler life.

However, a certain household disorganization persisted: Holly and I still went to school with our green wool uniform skirts shiny from wear and lack of dry cleaning, our saddle shoes remained scuffed, and our white socks dingy. Mamama had taught me to sew, so our uniform blouses weren't missing buttons, but I always wondered how my schoolmates at Laurel managed to keep their uniforms looking so clean, their blouses so fresh.

I had learned to run the automatic washer and dryer in the basement, but the laundry room itself soon became littered with dryer lint and spills of powdered detergent. None of us was bothered enough to sweep it up.

"Mom, the zipper on my uniform skirt is busted. Do we have any safety pins around?" I asked one morning.

"You know, Jack, I can't be responsible for everything! Why didn't you tell me the zipper was broken?" Her voice was taking on a familiar tone of frustration.

"Well, it just happened. I was only asking where I could find—"

"Damn it. I'm doing the best I can!" She was on the verge of tears of self-reproach.

"Mom, come on. I just . . ." With words failing me, and not wanting to cause a crying jag, I headed upstairs in search of a pin.

The "heavy work" my mother had always fretted over still had her stymied here at the Chesterland house. A weekly cleaning lady attended to housework. But the heavy work, anything that might be considered a man's work, generally went undone. Burnt out light bulbs hung in their sockets, broken hinges clung to door jams, leaky faucets dripped. They were daily reminders of and, in some odd way, protests against her husbandless state. As though having no man in the house was a badge of honor that made acceptable the neglect of maintenance chores. "You see, I don't have a man around. I refuse to cope," she seemed to be saying.

Some nights after dinner she took a hot bath, came down in her nightgown and bathrobe, and joined Holly and me as we watched *The George Gobel Show*. "Jack, give your old mother a foot rub, will you?" she said one night. She settled back on the couch, her feet in my lap. My fingers massaged her shiny soles, the rough heels and sharply creased toes. I relished the presence of my mother bathed and relaxed, the fragrance of her Ponds cold cream soothing the complaints and tempers of the day.

One day, a man entered my mother's life. An old beau of hers from her debutante days in the 1930s, perhaps recently divorced, he sought to re-kindle their romance. He took my mother out to dinner one night, and soon they were courting.

Kirke Lincoln had preserved his youthful nickname "Minkie." My mother for some reason instructed us to call him "Uncle," though he was no relation. A Cleveland bank manager for years until a bad heart had forced him to retire, he soon became a frequent visitor to the house.

I am not sure how my mother and Minkie came to reconnect, but he had apparently made an appearance some years earlier. According to my cousin Jeanie's memory of an incident at the West Hill Drive house, she and Marian were awakened late one night by loud voices downstairs (Holly and I must have been away or sound asleep). They crept down to find a strange man, Minkie, staggering around the house looking for his hat. Our mother kept telling him he'd come with no hat but, quite drunk, he insisted his hat was there and kept searching for it. Roused by the disturbance, David and our cousin Eric appeared wielding a broom and a fireplace poker to confront the intruder. This sent Jeanie and Marian into a fit of giggles. Finally my mother persuaded Minkie to leave, and everybody had laughed themselves silly at the bizarre intrusion.

When my mother and Minkie were dating, Holly and I observed him carefully. At dinners out—we were sometimes invited along on their dates—I studied this odd, stoop-shouldered man. As he attempted to engage us in dinner conversation, I came to worry if he had some sort of malady. He listened to us with a tilt of his head and spoke with slurred speech out of one side of his mouth. A nervous tic, a blinking of his eyes as if to fend off cigarette smoke, added to his peculiarity, and I wondered what my mother saw in him. But she was very vivacious on those evenings; her smiling and flirting with her beau gave us a fresh perspective on the irritable woman we had often witnessed.

Apart from Minkie's physical peculiarities—we learned they were caused by deafness in one ear as a result of childhood diphtheria—he seemed a kind, gentle person and very loving towards my mother. It appeared he was someone she could depend on, and her moods were much improved. He showed interest in Holly's and my activities and got along with other members of the family. So within a few months he and my mother were married in a quiet family ceremony in Mamama's living room.

I looked forward to my mother having a man with whom she could travel and enjoy a life beyond raising her children. And maybe, I thought, Minkie would take on some of the "heavy work." I could breathe a sigh of relief, no longer the uneasy witness to her tears and ragged tempers. On the other hand, I would miss our shared evenings of foot rubs in front of the TV.

Since Uncle Minkie had re-entered her life, my mother had begun to make visits to the beauty parlor and bought herself some stylish new outfits. Minkie taught Holly and me to play backgammon and one summer treated us to a trip to Disneyland. On our annual spring vacations to Delray Beach, we enjoyed the refreshing change of a man's company. Someone besides my mother could arrange outings and pay restaurant checks.

Though retired, Uncle Minkie dressed in a baggy gray business suit every weekday and drove to his club in downtown Cleveland. There he lunched, drank martinis, and played backgammon with his cronies through the afternoon. When he got home, he and my mother had a couple of rounds of cocktails before we all sat down to dinner. Having a man at one end of the table where none had ever been felt peculiar. Nodding and smiling through each meal, Minkie seemed more like a permanent guest than head of the household.

After a year or so, Uncle Minkie's slurred speech and quirky eye blinking, both exaggerated when he'd been drinking, prompted us to refer to him behind his back as "Uncle Blinkie." Often he sat in the living room, his fleshy hands resting on the arms of an easy chair, staring out at the back yard. His heart condition, it turned out, precluded any heavy lifting or yard work. But my mother, impatient with his lassitude, tried to roust him from his chair with suggestions of chores that needed doing. He answered her with smiley grunts and "yeps," indicating his lack of interest in "heavy work," which exasperated her.

"Minkie, I need you to set up the barbeque on the back patio," she said one summer day.

"Well, dear, I don't know . . ." his voice trailed off.

"Then, could you run to the hardware store for a screwdriver and some light bulbs?" He stared into space. Either he hadn't heard or had no inclination toward such things.

My mother groaned and grabbed her purse. "All right, *I'll* make the trip to the goddamn hardware store!"

"Yep, knew you would," murmured Uncle Minkie, folding his hands in his lap.

Over the years such scenes became commonplace, marked by his passivity and her nagging. Defenseless against her caustic remarks, he sat placidly or stood and walked into another room.

"Jackie, how about a game of backgammon?" he often asked me.

"Sure," I said. Though I wasn't a fan of the game, I sat down to play. He seemed so lonely.

One day, at the end of our spring vacation in Delray Beach, it was apparent Uncle Minkie had somehow caused a foul-up in our return airline reservations. We found ourselves standing beside our suitcases, blistering heat rising off the airport tarmac, waiting for a specially chartered plane that failed to appear. Gone was my mother's relaxed mood, her smile and jokes we'd enjoyed during our time away from home. She was livid.

"How could you be so stupid not to check those plane tickets?" she said to him. Silent, Uncle Minkie shifted his weight from side to side and squinted at the empty sky, as though his eyes could draw the overdue plane to us. My mother pulled on her cigarette and exhaled an angry cloud of smoke.

For some reason I felt it was up to me to ease the tension, "Never mind," I piped up, "at least this gives us a few extra hours in Florida! Ha-ha!"

"What the hell do you know about it?" Her voice was a whiplash. She glared at me. "Stop being such a *goddamn* Pollyanna!" She tossed her cigarette to the pavement, stamped and ground it out.

Stung with shame, I turned away as hot tears slid down my cheeks. This is what my mother truly thought of me. She hated me. For I had committed the worst sin imaginable. I'd tried to assuage her misery. Suddenly it became crystal clear that my mother *wanted* to be angry and miserable, and she despised me for my interference.

The little charter plane finally arrived and carried us to wherever we needed to be that day. And I was transported to a new awareness of where I stood in my mother's eyes.

My mother and Minkie often engaged in after-dinner drinking long after I'd done my evening homework and gone to bed. One night angry voices in the living room startled me awake. I tiptoed to the top of the stairs and listened. My hands and feet turned to ice as shouts and accusations studded with foul language flew up the stairs.

The clanking of a fireplace poker being pulled from its rack and my mother's cries of "Help, children, help!" spurred me to run down to the living room. I found her wielding the poker and Uncle Minkie staggering and trying to grab it from her.

"Mom, stop!" I cried. She looked at me as though I was some sort of intruder. A glint in her eye then told me she was enjoying the high drama being played out. But hadn't she cried for help? I stood in my nightgown feeling like a fool, as the odd seriocomic scene continued, Mom waving the poker about, Uncle Minkie cursing and tottering.

I thought someone was going to get hurt. I ran upstairs to call the police, who soon came to break up the peculiar altercation. "You're going to sleep this one off at the station, tonight, sir," said the officer ushering Uncle Minkie out the door.

By this time Holly had joined us, her face white with panic. "All right, girls, let's get to bed," my mother said, running her fingers through her hair and cutting off any discussion of what had just occurred. We traipsed back to our rooms. The next morning Uncle Minkie returned home, and life went on as before.

After that night I was always on guard for aggressive behavior from Uncle Minkie, but, as far as I know, that night's ruckus was never repeated. Most often "Blinkie" was merely the butt of family jokes, until his behavior ceased to be funny. A licensed pilot, he took to renting a Cessna and flying off for days at a time with no word as to why or where he was going. One day he returned from a jaunt to Mexico where he'd bought a dozen pairs of cowboy boots, sizes and colors chosen at random, intended as gifts for the whole family. We feigned delight at the boots, but his bizarre behavior had us worried.

My mother, frustrated with his erratic conduct, insisted Uncle Minkie see a doctor, who, after much testing, diagnosed him as manic-depressive. Soon medications tamped down my stepfather's mania, and revocation of his pilot's license put an end to his zany adventures. But he dropped into a passive state from which he couldn't be pulled. For days on end he sat in the living room armchair, smiling amiably, looking around for someone he could challenge to even one game of backgammon.

Several years later, after I'd married and moved to the East Coast, Uncle Minkie developed stomach cancer. He suffered for months and died a painful death. I went home for the memorial service with thoughts of trying to comfort my mother. But, characteristically stoic, she rejected my awkward gestures of sympathy. During the funeral, she shed no tears.

After the service she, Marian, Holly, and I went out to lunch. My mother seemed little disturbed by the death of her husband of fifteen years. She talked and quipped and laughed as usual. It wasn't until she was paying the bill for lunch that her trembling fingers and an uncommon shakiness in calculating the tip told me she was grieving. She was mourning deeply. And she was perhaps feeling frightened and lost at the prospect of life without Uncle Minkie. At sixty-four years old and with all of her children out of the house, my mother, for the first time in her life, was facing life at home utterly alone.

I had come to see my mother's marriage to Uncle Minkie as one fraught with frustration and disappointment, but perhaps I had it all wrong. Perhaps those days with him had been the best fifteen years of her life.

15
A QUEST

It all started with Mr. Adams, my fifth grade teacher, my first crush. I looked up from my spelling test to admire his handsome face and close-cropped hair similar to my dad's. It seemed to me Mr. Adams thought I was something special, perhaps because I was a good speller. Or maybe he thought I was pretty. Whichever it was, Mr. Adams was my first awareness of how it felt to be admired by a member of the opposite sex.

As a child I dreamed of one day marrying somebody like my dad, someone tall and blond, handsome and tan. But as I got older, it seemed those tall good-looking guys were never around for me. And—as my mother so often reminded me—neither was Dad.

At age fourteen I won the role of Josephine in a community theatre production of *H.M.S. Pinafore,* my first play, my first lead role. Performing on stage felt totally natural to me, and the fun of working with other teens was a new adventure. I found boys there, too, boys who seemed to really like me.

One of them was Paul. He was a fellow singer in our church choir and portrayed my father in *Pinafore.* Talented, smart, and headed for the Ivy League, Paul had great boyfriend potential. Had he been a few years younger, I might have danced with him at Mrs. Ford's Dancing School in the ballroom of the Alcazar Hotel.

Mrs. Ford's was where "young ladies" destined to be debutantes made the acquaintance of—and were permitted limited physical contact with—boys in the appropriate social class. Though Marian, Jeanie, David, and Susan had all done their time at Mrs. Ford's, I had balked at the idea.

"Mom," I'd pleaded, as I stood outside her closed bathroom door, "do I *have* to go to dancing school?" I dreaded the prospect of straining to talk to boys who were total strangers, whom I would probably hate, and none of whom would ever ask me to dance.

"Yes, you have to go," my mother insisted through the door.

I stood in the hall and tried to think of a way to weasel out of this predicament.

"But, Mom, it'll be horrible. I'll be taller than most of the boys and —"

"Jack, I don't want to discuss it. You're going to Mrs. Ford's and that's all there is to it." The toilet flushed. I was sunk.

That Friday evening dancing school was as dreadful as I'd imagined. I wore an ill-fitting satiny dress, patent leather shoes that pinched my toes, and white cotton gloves I yanked at continuously to accommodate my large hands. I sat with the other thirteen-year-old girls in a row of chairs along the perimeter of the ballroom, feeling the archetypal wallflower. As couples were dancing, the boys smirked, giggled, and exchanged smart-aleck remarks across the room.

At last a boy who was four feet tall and had the tiniest face and hands I'd ever seen approached and asked me to dance. As he struggled to lead me through the box step, I held myself as far from him as I could, my big gloved hand on his petite shoulder. Neither of us spoke or looked at each other during the entire dance.

Other equally miserable Friday evenings ensued. The instructor, Mr. Clancy, who saw me as a competent dancer, often chose me when he needed a partner to demonstrate the intricacies of the tango or the swing. I was flattered to be selected and felt at ease in the arms of Mr. Clancy, but attempting to waltz or fox trot with any of the churlish boys in class was torture. The boys at Mrs. Ford's, whom Mamama might have considered "suitable," were of no interest to me.

Paul, my fellow thespian, after we'd finished our weekend run of *Pinafore*, asked me out on a date. On the appointed evening he showed up right on time. My mother entertained him in the living room; I was upstairs rushing to repair the slice I'd carved from my shin as I struggled to shave my legs. At last I made my appearance, Band-Aids and all. My mother looked at me and said, "Jack, what happened? Did you run into a lawnmower?" She laughed while I, sizzling with embarrassment, sat down to join their conversation. But she was doing fine on her own; she had turned on all her charm for Paul and, with a false inquiring expression on her face, was busy exuding witty, pseudo-intellectual remarks. I sat tugging at my cotton skirt to hide the Band-Aids, while she flirted with my date.

Paul was the boy my mother, and perhaps Mamama, would have liked me to hold on to. He was from the right family (his parents were pillars of the church and card-carrying members of the WASP elite), he had attended the appropriate dancing school, and he was destined to follow his father into the family law firm. I could have gone down that path with Paul. But as much as I enjoyed our puppy love and luscious kisses all summer long, when he returned from his first year at Yale, I found him staid, stodgy, and a little pompous. At fifteen I was too young for that; I was ready for adventure.

I ended up dating a string of boys, all of them misfits of one sort or another—a country club brat with homicidal tendencies, a 22-year-old German emigrant my mother found acceptable because he was a church member, a mechanic's helper with a slick black hair comb, and others all equally unsuitable. I enjoyed their attentions, but my mother seldom approved; through warnings, sly hints, and ridicule, she subtly discouraged me from getting too close to any of them.

"A boy like that is dangerous," she'd warn. Or, "Well, you don't let him . . . kiss you . . . or anything . . . do you?" she'd ask, forcing me to lie. Or "Dear, don't you think he's a bit swishy?" she'd inquire with a laugh.

The fact was I had no idea what to do with boys. Sheltered by Laurel School from male contact and having no father at home, I didn't know what to look for in a boyfriend. I did find boys, however, to be the source of a magical feeling: with them I was valued, loved and desired.

The grievances I'd heard as I was growing up always trailed behind me. "Your father beat the hell out of me every time I got pregnant!" my mother had said, a suggestion that loving the wrong man—or any man—might end in disaster. "Your father was just plain rotten!" rang in my head, too. But I resisted allowing her words to dissuade me from going out with—and falling a little bit in love with—just about any boy who asked me.

As my teens progressed, I gravitated toward the world of the theatre—or "the *thee-ah-tah*" as my mother liked to call it. A friend at Laurel convinced me to take a bit part in a teen theatre production of *Bye Bye Birdie*, and soon I was playing supporting roles, then leads, in many of the musicals we performed during the year. The after-school rehearsals were more fun than I'd ever imagined. For the first time in my life I acquired a set of warm, wacky, talented friends. That and the magic of the theatre—singing, dancing, and wrapping myself in an alternate reality—seduced me and held me tight.

In summer our teenage troupe performed at an outdoor amphitheatre in downtown Cleveland known as Cain Park. Over the course of two summers I garnered the leads in The *Music Man, Guys and Dolls,* and *The King and I.* My mother, while far from being a pushy stage mom, was delighted the singing lessons she'd insisted on were paying off; she never missed an opening night.

"Jack, you were wonderful!" she cried at the end of each performance, flinging her arms around me for a quick hug. My mother thought I was wonderful. Wow.

I spent those two summers at Cain Park dazzled by the adulation of my peers, falling in love with the role of actress and the admiration of audiences. I was careful, however, not to introduce any boys from my theatre crowd to my mother, fearing her ridicule. I was learning to keep my boyfriends to myself.

When I went away to DePauw, I joined the elite theatre subculture, the only group into which I fit on that white-bread campus. I won the lead in the first play I auditioned for, and spent most of my four years in the theatre building. I dated a few college guys, but very few. I had come to accept myself as a non-conformist, a social misfit who didn't care about having a date every Saturday night. I concentrated on my studies, dazzled my peers with my mercurial Pegeen Mike in *Playboy of the Western World* and captured the admiration of my School of Music friends in the title role of *Carmen.* After four years, I headed home convinced that only a life in the theatre would provide me with the love and admiration I sought.

My parade of dreadful boyfriends, each of them more peculiar than the last, must have amused my mother. And perhaps irked her. At some point she threw out all the letters I'd received from various male admirers. When I rummaged around her attic searching for those testaments of love and affection, I found they had disappeared.

16

THE BIG APPLE

I sat in my senior acting class and listened to Dr. Elrod query us about our expectations after earning our B.A.'s in Speech and Theatre from DePauw University.

"Clearly," he chuckled, crossing his legs in a prissy, self-satisfied manner, "if you people have any intentions of being professional actors, you've been at the wrong school. You should have spent the last four years at Northwestern."

The other students and I all chortled along with him, implying our understanding that, as talented as we had proven ourselves to be in our high school and college productions, we would certainly not consider ourselves qualified for a professional acting career. But while I smiled at his remark, a dart of panic shot through me. For wasn't that what I was intending to do after graduation? Become an actress in New York City?

Acting and singing should surely be my profession, I thought. For what else was I trained? Hadn't I performed leads in all the teen and college plays? Hadn't I cut my teeth on summer stock in Ohio and on Cape Cod? And hadn't my mother told me how talented I was? Professional theatre was my destiny. So what was Dr. Elrod saying—that I should abandon my dream and become a teacher like him?

After graduation, with Dr. Elrod's words still buzzing in my brain, I spent a year back home to ponder my future. I moved out of my mother's house and shared an apartment with a girlfriend. That year I performed two leads at a semi-professional interracial theatre known as Karamu and sang the demanding role of Magda in Menotti's opera, *The Consul*. These successes solidified my determination to become a professional actress. But I knew that to have an actual career in the theatre, I'd need to develop it in New York City. Unfortunately, I was too much of a coward to venture there on my own.

Then I met Ken. My director for one of the Karamu plays, he was the first professional I'd worked with. Amazingly smart, intuitive and funny, he thoroughly charmed me. We began going out for drinks after rehearsals, and soon we became lovers. At the end of that year, Ken, who had earlier formed contacts with Broadway producers, planned to venture off to New York to solidify his career. This was my chance.

After I'd introduced them, my mother got along with Ken—his humor and intellect kept pace with hers—but she resisted the idea of my taking off for New York with him. "Dear, New York is a perfectly *wretched* place!" she said, lending as much drama to this statement as possible. Though it seemed unlikely she'd spent more than an overnight in New York as an embarkation point for a cruise with Uncle Minkie, she spoke as though she were an expert.

"And, furthermore, I don't want you living with Ken. It's unseemly." Her choice of words implied a little joke, but she had no intention of letting her unmarried daughter take up residence with a man. I feared that Ken being Jewish might have had something to do with her objection.

"Come on, Mom, you like Ken. He knows his way around New York, and he'll watch out for me. I'll be fine. You've always encouraged my acting and my singing. This is the only way for me to make the most of my talent. I've got to do this if I'm going to be a professional."

"Oh, Lord, if only everyone would do exactly as I say!" One of her characteristic humorous remarks, this time it held no levity.

"Come on, Mom!"

"Jack, I said '*No!*'" She was furious. "I don't want you going off with that . . . MAN!" I could tell she'd wanted to say "that JEW" but had bit her tongue.

"Mom, I'm twenty-three years old! This is my chance and I'm taking it!" I marched off to pack my bags.

So, in November of 1969, Ken and I headed for the Big Apple. Our first apartment, which we struggled for weeks to find, was a sublet on West Thirteenth Street. We snagged it only because the woman subletting it happened to be an alumna of Laurel School. A musty third-floor studio, just one cramped room with a cooking range and a tiny refrigerator on one wall, the flat was furnished with a little drop-leaf dining table and a rickety trundle bed in the corner. In the Chinese red bathroom, flakes of plaster threatened to snow from the ceiling. The only window faced a dismal airshaft, providing an aura of perpetual gloom.

As I bathed one evening in the bathroom's claw-foot tub, contemplating how I would get up the courage to make phone calls to my meager list of contacts, pull together professional photos and a resume, and actually venture out to auditions, a cockroach scooted along the edge of the tub next to my left eye. He stopped to survey my naked body. I pulled a washcloth across my chest. With the waggling of his antennae, he seemed to be warning me to let him pass unharmed—"I'm tougher than you, don't even THINK about swatting me!"—then scuttled off to the kitchen counter to find a meal.

Ken soon found work, but it was a stage-managing job in Toronto, so he departed, and I was left alone. I took a deep breath and started making the rounds to auditions and interviews. Most of them were "cattle calls" where I was one of hundreds of young hopefuls who stood for hours in drafty, dark hallways or grubby rehearsal studios or along the streets in front of Broadway theatres, waiting to be seen. I grasped my portfolio with sweaty fingers, anticipating how I would present myself to the producer or director of a show and perhaps get a chance to sing, dance, or read for a part. I stood mute as other aspirants—all of whom I assumed to be far more experienced than I—compared notes on what agents might be seeing new people, what parts were probably pre-cast, and other tidbits of gossip in the auditioning scene. I signed up for voice lessons, acting school, and dance classes, which put me in touch with many fellow actors, all struggling to get a handle on a career. Making a few friends helped buoy my confidence.

A tall, slender, almost-pretty girl with long, shining tresses, I walked miles up and down the streets and avenues of Manhattan, stopping in at agents' and producers' offices to drop off my picture and resume. I sported a breezy smile as I made my rounds, but inside anxiety churned. The recognition of my talent I so eagerly sought was hard-won. After several months of snagging nothing but a part in a children's show, humiliation also began to seep into my consciousness. To have to work so hard just to get a chance to be seen or heard by a casting director felt like begging. Even when I did land a good interview or an audition, I knew rejection was not only possible but likely. The trick, I was advised, was to avoid internalizing the rebuff. Seemed easy enough. *I have to be tough-skinned to make it in this business*, I told myself. *I have to pay my dues.* So I kept on walking.

Making rounds and taking classes exhausted me, but maneuvering around New York City in 1970 was itself a daunting experience. The rolling landscape of Gates Mills, Ohio, and the cornfields of Greencastle, Indiana, hadn't prepared me for the frenzied avenues of Manhattan. The routes of the subways and busses confounded me, and the streets harbored filth and danger. When I wasn't dodging litter, dog shit, and leaking garbage bags strewn along every sidewalk, I faced confrontation with homeless people and potential purse-snatchers at every corner. The areas I frequented for auditions, around Eighth Avenue and Forty-second Street, were lined with topless bars and peep-shows.

The walk to auditions presented a repulsive obstacle course punctuated by construction workers' wolf whistles and panhandlers' entreaties, leaving me unnerved and fretful by the time I reached an audition. Once at the appointed rehearsal hall, I would have only a few minutes to shirk all the distractions, pull myself together, become thoroughly engaging, and pour out my heart in song.

My phone calls home to my mother were fraught with nervous assurances that things were going well. "No, Mom, I haven't gotten a part yet, but I had a great audition yesterday for an off-off-Broadway play. I'm waiting to hear back." I had no idea what her expectations were, but I didn't want to unnerve her with bad news. Nor could I let her think my sojourn to the big city with "that . . . MAN" was for naught. As my singing was the one thing she loved about me, I knew I had to keep at it and make those voice lessons she'd given me pay off.

"Well, do you need money, dear?" my mother asked during each call. " I can send you whatever you need."

"No, Mom, I'm fine." I was living on my savings and a bequest from Mamama. I had no particular worries about money. I merely wanted an acting job to prove I was as talented as everyone at home had thought me to be. And I wouldn't accept my mother's money in any event; attached to it would be an unspoken obligation: to leave Ken, ditch the "wretched" city and come home.

"Don't worry about me, Mom, really. Something will turn up," said the smiling Pollyanna she knew so well. Inside my heart was bursting with doubt and fear, but sharing my feelings with her was too risky. It might upset her equilibrium to know I wasn't the patient, self-reliant girl she'd taught me to be. And actually verbalizing my insecurities would unnerve me, as well.

"Well, just do the best you can, dear. That's all you can do." I acknowledged her words, but clinging to my subconscious was the haunting phrase I had heard so often when I was growing up: "You'll never be Number One, dear."

I spent a lot of time in my apartment, mainly to avoid the noise and chaos of the city streets. Ken was often out of town with a show he was stage managing or directing, so I was on my own, trying to piece together some kind of life. One evening at dusk, I sat on the floor of my apartment in my tights and sweatshirt, performing an exercise assigned by my acting teacher. As instructed, I spoke into a tape recorder to explore my deepest feelings. When I rewound the tape and hit "Play," the sound of my sorrowful voice, expressing my insecurities and profound loneliness, reduced me to a flood of tears. I lay back on the hardwood floor, blinking at the chalky white ceiling. *This is too painful. What in god's name am I doing here?*

I couldn't share any of this with my mother. She'd be too disappointed.

My mother visited from Chesterland occasionally. She loathed cities and was out of her element in the Big Apple, so I knew I had to provide activities to make her feel at ease and keep her entertained.

On her first visit—in 1970 when I'd been living in the city for about six months—I reserved a room for her at the Gramercy Park Hotel. It was near my new apartment on Lexington and Twenty-third and had as one of its many luxury amenities the beautiful, and very exclusive, Gramercy Park. She'd love this small elegant accommodation, I felt, and the park's charming patch of greenery in the drab cityscape would surely please her.

I got her settled into the hotel, but she seemed unimpressed with the beautifully decorated room she'd been given. "A bit stuffy, isn't it, dear?" she said as she struggled to yank up a window sash.

"Mom, leave that! The bellman can take care of it. Let's go see the park!"

In the park I commented on the wondrous pink and white flowering dogwoods, such a stark contrast to the neglected street trees dotted along Lexington Avenue. "Marvelous, aren't they, Mom?"

"My trees at home are so slow, they're just leafing out." she replied. We ambled along, and I marveled at the colorful tulips and early blooming perennials before us. "Mom, look at those primroses, aren't they gorgeous?" She wandered away from me down the path, sat on a bench, pulled a Kleenex from her bag and blew her nose.

"This garden is amazing, isn't it?" I said, trying to engage her in the greenery surrounding us.

"When I get home, I have to get the gardeners to dig up my vegetable garden. I simply can't do it myself anymore. Of course, those Bryce boys always do a lousy job, and they charge me an arm and a leg, but who else can I get?"

"Mom," I persisted, "look at that little fountain. Isn't that charming?" The stone garden feature burbled.

"If I don't get the tomato plants in soon, it'll be September before I see any fruit," was her reply.

Later she took me out to lunch and shopping. I wanted to show her the big city stores, and she expressed a desire to buy me things for the apartment, to put her stamp on my new lifestyle.

Days earlier I had made a reservation at Luchow's for dinner. A hearty old-fashioned German restaurant, very popular at the time, especially with tourists, the restaurant was having its May Wine Festival featuring the music of a Vienna string quartet during dinner. I was sure this place would amuse her no end, as there was nothing comparable in Cleveland.

My brother David was in New York then, divorced and living alone, working as an executive at ABC. I'd called to ask him to join us for dinner.

"David, Mom's going to be in town this weekend. I made a reservation at Luchow's."

He ignored my news. "Jacq, I got the check from Dad for my birthday." His remark carried the snide tone I knew so well.

"Oh, really, what are you going to do with it?" I asked, aware I was automatically aping his sarcastic timbre. David had become very successful at ABC—fake-vomit-on-desk-chair-pranks notwithstanding; I knew he had no use for our father's customary twenty-five dollar check.

"I tore it up," said David.

"What?"

"I tore it up and tossed it in the trash. What a fucking insult! Twenty-five dollars? What does he think I am? Is that some kind of payoff for being such a shit father?"

I didn't follow David's logic—I suspected there was none—but I wasn't going to argue. It occurred to me he might be in therapy, working through parent issues.

"Well, anyway," I plowed on, "Mom will be here Friday. Meet us Saturday at Luchow's at seven. It's on West Fourteenth. OK?"

"I'm not coming."

"What?"

"I have better things to do than listen to her constant bitching."

"David, I told her you were coming!" My mother's visit was ostensibly to see me, inspect my new apartment, and learn how my career was progressing, but I suspected she was more looking forward to seeing David. Bad boy that he was, his cleverness and wit were irresistible to her. During our phone calls she always asked, "How's David?" "Have you heard anything from David?" or "What's David up to? He never answers my letters." So it was important he make an appearance at dinner.

"David, you have to come!" I cried.

"I don't have to do a fucking thing! No."

I begged for a while and then gave up. I knew if I laid low and called to remind him at the last minute, I'd likely find him in a better mood and he'd reconsider.

Saturday night came, and David did show up at Luchow's. My mother and I were listening to the string quartet in the dark-paneled room draped with grape vines. As she didn't seem to find the atmosphere in the least bit amusing, I tried to entertain her with stories about my life in New York. I was unable to tell her the truth, so I expounded on my latest audition adventures, trying to make them seem more intriguing than they actually were.

"Well, the choreographer was the MOST peculiar looking person . . ." I blathered on. Soon David's appearance interrupted.

"Hi, dear!" cried my mother. Suddenly, for the first time since her arrival in New York, joy filled her voice, and a huge smile came over her face. She proffered her cheek toward him for a kiss. David ignored her gesture and sat down.

"How have you been, dear?" The thrill of seeing him glowed in her eyes. "You look so thin!"

He turned to me. "Jacq, what are you drinking?"

"Gin and tonic," I replied. *Uh-oh.* "David, aren't you going to say hello to your mother?"

A waiter presented himself.

"I'll have a gin and tonic. Thank you," David said and turned his gaze to a slender blonde passing our table.

"Jack and I had quite a day today," said my mother. "We went to Central Park, then lunch and shopping. I never knew Bloomingdales was so huge! I was absolutely exhausted . . . "

David turned away from her, folded his arms, lifted his chin and stared off into space. So that was it, I thought—the silent treatment. Some ancient rage, some long-festering resentment, was apparently burning inside him. It probably had to do with the night twenty years earlier when, intoxicated and exhausted, she had humiliated him by throwing his teenaged girlfriend out of the West Hill Drive house. Whatever the problem was, David had chosen silence as his weapon of revenge.

"David, Mom's talking to you!" I tried to get him to come around.

"I don't care what she's doing," he declared, a sans-souci lilt to his voice. "When can we order?" He flipped open his menu, glanced at the contents, then tossed it onto the table.

My mother knew what he was up to. They had had their feuds through the years—our childhood summers were punctuated by sharp arguments ending with David stomping out of the house and peeling up the gravel driveway—but his determined rudeness now was extreme. It seemed she felt her only defense was to bait him, as she proceeded to pepper him with a rapid-fire series of questions and remarks, to show she resented his behavior but would continue with her half of the conversation in spite of him.

"Well, dear, how's your work?" Silence. "Fine, it appears." David buttered his roll. "Are you coming to the Cape this summer? . . . You have to let me know, so I can reserve a room for you." Our annual family trip to Cape Cod was a common source of dialogue, but David wasn't biting. Then, "What do you want for Christmas?" This last was a silly question, though provocative, as David invariably answered it with a sharp "Nothing!" However, this time he sat in stony silence, barely looking at her.

"So, you've decided not to speak. Rather childish, isn't it? And rude, considering I came all the way from Cleveland to see my children . . . You are behaving like an ass, you know . . . "

This interplay between them became the focal point of the evening. Any stories I had saved up to tell about my New York City escapades were shunted aside in favor of their acrimony. I attempted to interject a few comments. "Mom, just ignore him. Are you enjoying your dinner?" But she sidestepped my remark. She was intent on one thing only: forcing him to speak to her.

I chewed my Weiner Schnitzel while they stabbed at their steaks and ordered more drinks. She continued to attack him, her words becoming louder and more biting. "You are just like your father—selfish! Rotten!" Sipping my gin and tonic, I tried to lose myself in the sweet-sour fragrance of sauerbraten and the lilting sound of the Vienna string quartet, but my insides seethed. I was caught in the crossfire and being by-passed to boot, and of course this mess was of my own doing.

After his third drink, David had had enough. He threw down his napkin and stomped out of Luchow's without so much as a "Good night." He had won.

I turned to her. "I'm sorry, Mom. I have no idea what that was all about."

A pool of tears had stalled along the lower lids of her deep brown eyes. I cast about for something to say to assuage the hurt. "How about an after-dinner drink, Mom?" She did not answer me but stared out at where David had left the room. "How about a stinger?"

Over the next few years I landed a fair amount of work in the theatre: chorus parts in a couple of pre-Broadway shows, a few commercials, some work in films as an extra, a bit on a TV sitcom, an off-Broadway show or two, and some leading roles in summer stock musicals. They were fun, all these jobs, and each added a tiny lift to my ego, but the engagements were sporadic and didn't add up to anything of substance. I came to feel that after years of effort I had failed to advance beyond the role of dime-a-dozen hopeful, merely one of the thousands of New York City unemployed actors.

I kept myself busy with some temporary clerical work in Manhattan offices, and I waitressed a bit, to earn a little money and because it was what unemployed actresses did. But having no structure in my life made me miserable. I felt I was floating in a murky space in which I did not belong, casting my gaze for something solid to hold on to. I continued listlessly with my voice lessons, my acting and dance classes, and I hid in my apartment. Even when Ken was home, his warm presence filling our little apartment, he was so busy with appointments and rehearsals, I felt very alone. I looked to his work and his colorful friends for sustenance, but living vicariously off his success was unsatisfying.

Occasionally Ken and I visited some friends of his in Connecticut to get a break from the city. The trees, sunlight, lovely homes and gardens we encountered refreshed us and gave glimpses of what our life could be. Returning to New York after these weekends I came to realize how the city's persistent stench of garbage and dog shit, the sight of crazies on every street corner, the incessant unnerving noise, were driving me insane.

After five years of a ragged roller coaster ride in the world of the theatre, I had to question if what I'd accomplished was a meaningful body of work, if this was the career I'd envisioned, and if the effort to get recognition of my talent, and my self, was worth it. Did all the bits and bobs of theatrical excitement amount to anything? Where was the admiration and love I'd craved?

I shared my anxieties with Ken but, absorbed in his own burgeoning career, he offered little solace. His reluctance to comment on my lack of success told me all I needed to know. I caved in to the idea that, despite my talent, I didn't possess the drive, the "chutzpah" to succeed in the theatre. The self-confidence required to become the leading lady I had dreamed of—the next Barbara Cook—eluded me. And as thirsty as I was for love, the vessel I envisaged to be holding it remained stubbornly out of reach.

As the harsh demands on my emotional resilience wore me down, I thought of that cocky cockroach on the rim of my bathtub on West Thirteenth Street. He had looked me over, and he'd seen it—I was no match for the New York theatre.

Ken and I married in 1974. Shortly after, I insisted that we move out of the City. I had had a great adventure, one that not many people get to experience, and I'd given it my best shot, but I'd had enough of the struggle. The trees and houses and gardens of Connecticut were calling to me. We both agreed Ken was at a point in his career where commuting to New York from the suburbs was feasible, and now a regional theatre in New Haven had offered him work. So we packed all our belongings and made our getaway.

My mother never commented on my failed career and whether or not she was disappointed. "Well, at least you're out of that wretched city!" she said.

The possibilities of a new life excited me. Ken and I found an apartment in Greenwich with high ceilings and bright windows. Before long I had a job as a performing arts administrator. And a new role: married lady in the burbs.

17

KEN

Ken and I married, oddly enough, as a result of a nudge from my mother. For five years he and I had juggled the idea of marriage back and forth, and I shared my thoughts with her.

"Mom," I said one spring day when I was visiting Chesterland, "Ken and I were thinking that if we got married, we'd love to do it right here, have the ceremony in this pretty back yard of yours." The landscape outside her living room window, young upright oak trees with rays of light beaming onto the grass beneath their canopies, seemed an idyllic setting for taking marriage vows.

"You two are getting married?" She raised her tufted eyebrows and flicked the ash from her cigarette.

"Well, no . . . I mean, yes, maybe. We're not sure yet. But it would be neat to have the wedding here, if we did, that's all." I didn't want to get her hopes up that her daughter, who'd been living in sin for five years, might actually legitimize the relationship.

The topic didn't resurface until a few weeks later when I was back in New York, and the phone rang. "Dear, your news about getting married really threw me for a loop. If you're going to have a wedding here," Mom said, "you have to let me know! I've got to call the caterer. Hough's gets booked months in advance!"

"Well, Mom, I don't know exactly . . . I'll talk to Ken and call you back."

The issue being forced in this peculiar way, he and I did talk about it, and decided, yes, this was the time. We'd been together five years, shared the ups and downs of career issues and personal problems, and we loved each other. Why not? We selected an October date, and I picked up the phone to let my mother know she could call Hough's.

The wedding, as it happened, had to take place indoors due to unceasing rain. A simple affair, family and a few friends, it was fraught with anxiety over the awkwardness of having Dad and Polly and Dad's mother (whom my mother detested) in the house. She and I had argued over where to seat them for dinner to be out of my mother's sight, and I'd been reduced to tears. Nevertheless, the little ceremony went as planned in my mother's powder-blue living room.

Nine years later, however, Ken and I found ourselves in a terrible place. Our marriage was torn with stress, tensions yanked at the underpinnings of our love, and one night the final blow was struck. When I rolled over to his side of the bed for a goodnight kiss, Ken, wide awake, groaned and edged away.

Stunned by the rejection, I shot back with, "If you can't do better than that, then just get out!"

"All right." His voice was flat, "I think I will."

I snapped off the light and clutched my pillow. *Is this it, then? Is he really going to leave?* We had quarreled before, but his abruptness felt final. My heart went hollow. I didn't really want my marriage to end, but I had told him to leave and now had to stand my ground. Holding my silence tight to my breast, I willed myself to sleep.

Over coffee the next morning Ken said he'd be gone when I got home from work. This was not unusual, as his late rehearsals often meant he spent nights at the apartments of friends in New York or New Haven. But this sounded different. He adjusted his horn-rimmed glasses with the knuckle of his index finger and ran a beefy hand over his mustache and beard. These familiar telltale gestures telegraphed he was skirting around some truth or harboring a hidden agenda, and alarms went off.

"So, is this it?" I asked. At this point I might as well voice what I was feeling. "Are you leaving for good? It's not really what *I* want, but if *you* do, then you should go." However, perhaps unwilling to accept the responsibility I was trying to foist onto him, he gave no answer. We parted that day, unsure what lay ahead.

When I got home from work that evening, I found a note on the kitchen counter.

> *I never thought of leaving for good. I am not thinking of it. After 14 years or whatever I got afraid of feeling myself slip back into the quiet dishonesty we have <u>both</u> been a party to. I want this to work out.*
>
> *Kenneth*

I pored over the note and tried to wrench meaning from every word. " . . .*14 years or whatever* . . ." Did he really not know how long we'd been together? " . . . *the quiet dishonesty we have <u>both</u>* . . ." But wasn't he the one who had proven himself to be the prevaricator, prone to lies and evasions? "*I want this to work out.*" From these final words I grasped a faint hope that I hadn't inadvertently pulled the plug on my marriage. But overall, the note spelled doom.

Our life in Connecticut had been a dream compared to the horrors of New York City, and with a job as a regional theatre manager, I'd found the structure I needed. Ken, whose charisma instilled confidence in actors and designers, had become quite a successful stage director. Though he was out of town directing plays for long stretches, I managed the solitude and assured myself we had a viable marriage in spite of the absences.

With his artistic genius and sense of humor and my practicality and self-reliance, we seemed to complement each other perfectly. We went to the theatre often, socialized with talented actors and artists, traveled to California, England, and France, and had many, many fun times. Having no children gave us a great deal of freedom. We were comfortable together, and I loved him very much.

Eventually I left non-profit theatre management and took a more stable job with a market research firm. I regretted being away from the arts, but I was able to maintain my connection to the theatre through Ken. However, during the nine years of our marriage, I came to see that I was very much on the periphery of his life. He the star surrounded by admirers, I the smiling tag-along wife standing on the sidelines, the arrangement had become lopsided. Our life together revolved around his work, and everything in our marriage took second place to his career. I kept waiting for him to put me first, waiting "like patience on a monument," as my mother had said when I was a child. But Ken was pre-occupied with his appointments and rehearsals and performance schedules, all of which took precedence over me. In the process my self-esteem got tapped down inch by inch without my realizing. My mother's caution, "You'll never be Number One, dear," may have also lurked in my subconscious.

Apart from the discomfort I felt being an observer, not a player, in his life, I struggled with Ken's need to dominate. Having learned to be autonomous in New York, I did not mind being alone for weeks at a time—I prided myself on my independence and self-sufficiency— but when Ken would return from one of his trips, an anxious period of adjustment ensued. While he was on the road, I became accustomed to making all the household decisions—much as my mother had always done with Uncle Minkie—but when he returned home, he could not accept my being in charge. He needed to re-gain control.

One evening, after fixing him a welcome-home dinner, I set about washing the dishes. He hovered over me. "Hey," he said, "you're going to break the dishwasher doing that."

"What?"

"The dishwasher is going to break if you load all the dishes on one side. It'll be out of balance. You're going to bust it."

"What!" It seemed to me I'd been loading the dishwasher for years up till now without any guidance or mishap.

"Look, this is the way you do it." And he proceeded to reload every dish according to his standards.

I stood aside in amazement. Though I wanted to say, "Get off my back, you jerk!" I didn't. For the hundredth time since we'd been together, I decided it was not worth rocking the boat and risking a fight, so I swallowed my feelings and let the incident pass. A side effect of the proverbial money, sex, and infidelity issues that had plagued us over the years, frequent squabbles such as this had created tensions that were driving us apart.

After studying Ken's enigmatic note on the kitchen counter, I went to my weekly choral rehearsal. The routine of warming up and singing Mozart normally gave me pure joy. But this night I could barely catch my breath to voice a note. My mind raced. *My husband has left me. I am going to be alone. Oh, god, I'm going to be just like my mother, alone.*

Over the next week Ken and I tiptoed around the issue of whether we had a future together. Then, from the safety of his borrowed apartment in New Haven, he finally admitted it: he had a girlfriend, a woman he'd been flirting with who was now his new love. With that admission, any glimmer of hope I might have had of dismissing our bedtime quarrel receded behind murky clouds.

I began a journal that night to capture my despair in words and to manage the fear. I wrote everything down—my humiliation, hurt, resentment, and anger—all feelings I'd never confronted in the nine years of our marriage. For many days and nights I wrote of my anguish, and found it oddly paired with an eagerness to be free of Ken's thoughtlessness and manipulation. I alternated between tears and rhapsody, was caught between chastising myself for losing a prize husband and being relieved, even joyous, that I might now escape Ken's self-absorption and neglect. This went on for weeks, and, though Ken and I spoke regularly on the phone, the confusion and uncertainty of whether or not I should fight for my marriage tortured me.

During this time, I shared my feelings with only a few friends, an amazing therapist whom Ken and I had been seeing together before our rift, and my journal. I did not confide in my mother. Her reaction would have been unthinkable. She would castigate Ken, I feared, implying "I told you so. You should *never* have gone off with him." Then she'd turn the blame onto herself; the conversation would become about her. "It's all my fault," she'd cry through her tears, "I was never a good enough mother!" thereby compounding my distress. Mostly I dreaded her severe disappointment that I, too, had failed in matrimony.

Up to that time I was the only member of our family who had held a marriage together. Marian, David, Jeanie, and Susan all had been divorced. Other than Holly, who had wisely remained single, I was the only one who had been immune to the family curse of divorce, and it was humiliating to know I had taken pride in that status, and that now my marriage, too, was holding on by a mere thread.

Before long Ken told me he'd moved in with his girlfriend. Horrified that he would do such a thing when we'd just separated, I protested. "How could you?" I cried.

"Isn't that all right?" he asked, as if I were a referee on the rules of marital separation.

He and I had countless heated conversations trying to sort out our feelings, but, hard as I tried, I could make no sense of the nightmare in which I was entangled. Daily, hourly, I faced the fear of abandonment, the shame of failure, and an inability to understand why my husband was hurting me so. Monday through Friday I managed my work at the office, but hours dragged on; days were endless. Confused and emotionally exhausted, I feared my body would succumb to some dreaded disease from all the stress.

One thing predominated our many discussions: Ken had become unhappy. The domesticity we had envisioned together in our cozy Connecticut cottage and my chatter about the lush flower garden I would create, now bored and threatened to suffocate him.

Again and again my mother's words—"Your father was rotten . . . he ran off with that woman . . ." streaked through my brain. I was determined, however, that if my marriage ended, I would not be like her. I would not succumb to such bitterness; I would find another way to manage the hurt. I worked diligently with my therapist to come to understand the dynamics of my marriage, the underlying reasons for Ken's behavior, and how I myself had inadvertently contributed to our relationship's downfall. The discoveries I made provided me great relief.

Cowards unable to face the consequences of our situation, Ken and I were both determined to keep the separation a secret from our families. If we told our parents what was occurring, that declaration would make it true—our marriage was coming to an end. Eventually, though, I had to tell my mother.

"Mom," I said into the phone, "I've got . . . some . . . look, I'm going to make this a very brief call. I just don't want to talk about it a lot." In the dim bedroom light my eyes traced the wavery wrinkles on the unmade bed. "But . . .well . . . Ken and I are separated. We've been having some problems. He's living in New York right now. But I'm fine. Don't worry about me."

"Oh, no." The shock and pain in her voice made me wince. However, she did not castigate Ken as I had dreaded. Instead, breathless because she knew I was rushing her off the phone, she said, "Well, you always have yourself, dear. Remember that, you always have yourself."

"I know, Mom, I know." I paused for a second. "I've got to go, Mom. Don't worry about me. I'll call you next week." I hung up the phone and surrendered to a torrent of tears. As perhaps did she.

"*You always have yourself.*" Of course. I did have myself to depend on. For hadn't she trained me, by example, to be self-reliant? Strong in the face of whatever trouble might find me?

When they found out about Ken and me separating, Marian, David, and Holly were all very supportive during those stressful days, as were Jeanie and Susan. And many friends I never even knew I had bolstered me, as well.

Then one evening I stumbled onto some good fortune. I met a man named George. A thoughtful, gentle, loving person, he made me laugh and gave me back my identity as an attractive woman. George, from our first meeting, earned the title "My Darling." Not only did he play a vital role in my struggle to rebuild my self-esteem, his patience and persistence in pursuit of our relationship, even through all my doubt and emotional turmoil, gave me hope for the future. Being loved this way was a whole new experience.

Nevertheless, for months Ken and I performed a macabre dance of advance and retreat. He wanted to leave the girlfriend and come home—but then he didn't; we thought we could understand each other's feelings—but then we couldn't; maybe we should try to come together again—but, no, we shouldn't, we had to end the marriage. Through all this vacillation, which caused me untold misery, an insistent strand of connective tissue—could it have been a deep-seated love and respect for each other, I wondered—seemed to bind Ken and me together, and it simply would not release.

Finally though, Ken and I went through a lengthy process of mediation, and we divorced on peaceable terms. We both had new lovers and expectations for a fresh start. Subjected to two years of acute stress, the tough connective tissue that had tethered us together—which may or may not have been love—finally snapped. And we were set free.

My traumatic experience of separation and divorce caused me to realize things about my mother I'd never considered. When she had divorced my father back in 1950, she had not been free. She'd had four children for whom she was solely responsible. And in an era when divorce was frowned upon, she'd had social stigma to contend with, as well. How had she seen her future? With the bewilderment and hurt she must have suffered, how did she manage?

My mother had had no career, no meaningful work to fall back on when her life was turned upside-down by her husband's desertion. How endless her hours must have seemed, with only the needs and complaints of her children to distract her from her distress. How did she get through her days?

And whom had she turned to for emotional support when her husband had left and her life had been torn apart? To her mother— so proper, cool and reserved? To Auntie Marian, who was herself severely depressed? My mother had had no patient psychotherapist to listen to her woes and assist in building her self-confidence. How did she survive, I wonder, with so little help?

18

NOT US

"So, we're sending her home. You see, there's nothing more the hospital can do for her," my mother's doctor told me.

I hung up the phone and stared into the cold, ashy fireplace in my mother's living room. I had listened, or tried to, as the doctor gave me a long-winded, technical description of the progression of her lung cancer. The words of the death sentence sped across my consciousness like a flock of starlings, barely taking hold. The only phrase that pierced through the cloud of my fear and confusion was "*metastasized to her brain*." I had had to ask the doctor to define "metastasize" but, after he did, that phrase was the only one I heard and clearly understood.

It had been the previous summer, when my mother, an otherwise healthy seventy-year-old, had begun to complain of a persistent pain on the side of her face. She had had a wracking cough as well, but that was normal for her. As she often caught colds and was "allergic" to air conditioning, her children were accustomed to that cough, the hacking and choking she seldom tried to hide. We made faint attempts to steer her away from her mentholated Kools, but she shunned our efforts.

Irritated that the doctors couldn't discern the cause of her facial pain, she was resigned to endure it. "It's all right about me, children," she said. But her uncommonly quiet mood and occasional winces—the jerk of a hand or trembling of an elbow—telegraphed her discomfort.

We were all together at the Lighthouse Inn on Cape Cod, an ocean resort we'd summered at every year since we were kids. Normally we'd be looking forward to dinner followed by a rousing game of "Ghost." My mother, a smart and crafty player, often spelled outrageous words and brought us to screams of laughter at her antics as she attempted to force us to speak to her when she was a "ghost."

But it seemed unlikely she'd feel up to playing our favorite game tonight. Marian, Holly, and I, and an assortment of grandchildren, were gathered in our mother's cabin for our customary five o'clock cocktail hour before dinner. Late afternoon sun cast shadows on the pine-paneled walls.

I took a sip of my gin and tonic. "Mom, did the doctor give you anything for the pain?" I asked.

"Yes, but it upset my stomach, and it didn't help anyway. I threw it out." She made a tossing gesture with her cigarette and gave a little chuckle.

"Mom, come on! Then see another doctor—" I said, annoyed by her familiar intractability.

"No, another doctor wouldn't know anything either. None of them do. They're all a bunch of 'ijjits.' It's all right . . ." A coughing spasm put an end to the conversation. Her body doubled over as she choked and sprayed sputum into a ragged Kleenex. I knew any further protests would irritate her and bring her to tears, so I held my peace. She finally recovered from her coughing bout. Then she wrapped her gauzy white shawl around her bronzed shoulders, and we all trailed across the lawn for dinner at the Inn.

Uncle Minkie had been dead for six years, and my mother had accustomed herself to living alone in Chesterland. Holly, Marian, my cousin Jeanie and various grandchildren were all close by in Cleveland to provide company, but by then I was living in Connecticut. The familiar "When are you coming home for a visit, dear? I'll pay for your trip," nagged at me. However, as often as I flew out to Cleveland to spend a few days, it never seemed to satisfy her.

On one visit, after arriving for a weekend and settling into the living room, I shared a few moments of lively conversation with her, newsy stuff that brought out her good spirits. "How's your friend Mrs. Shallenberger, Mom?"

"Oh, she's a laugh-riot, as always. We had lunch the other day . . ."

But soon her interest in our chat lagged, and she switched on the tiny TV at her elbow and took a sip of sherry. I'd lost her. I sat in an armchair wondering why I had traveled home at her request only to find myself shut out. A few days later, heading for the airport, I was hounded by angst that I hadn't spent the time well, that I hadn't connected with her, hadn't given her whatever it was she needed, and that the visit had been a waste. Maybe on the next trip home, I thought, I'll make it up to her. Maybe next time.

Tests to learn the cause of my mother's facial pain turned up what I'd feared and carefully stored at the back of my brain: lung cancer. Once the dreaded disease was diagnosed and she had begun radiation treatments, my guilt at not spending more time with her intensified. Marian and Holly were taking all the responsibility for her care; my absence seemed like cowardice. So I flew home whenever I could.

On a January visit I made an attempt to talk to her about her illness. She sat staring out her picture window, watching trails of snow drift from the steely sky and a pair of cardinals careen around the bird feeder. Her shock of gray hair brushed up and away from her high cheekbones, her swollen fingers grasping a cigarette, she seemed to be struggling to figure out what had gone wrong. She started to cough and couldn't stop. She choked until she nearly strangled. The offer of a glass of water, a slap on the back, or words of comfort would be summarily rejected, I knew, so I sat still, inwardly flinching with each hack.

Wiping tears from her cheeks with a Kleenex, she said, "It's all right. I've gotten used to it." She cleared her throat, swallowed, and regained her gaze out the window. After a few moments, she turned to me. "You know, I'm not afraid of dying. I'm not afraid of death, I'm really not. It's the pain. I'm just scared of the pain, that's all." She returned to her contemplation of the birds.

I held my silence, with the hope that simply listening was best. The ticking of the carriage clock on the mantelpiece filled the space between us. As always, a book lay open face-down on the couch beside her. Her eyes shifted from the window to her book. She fondled its cover, picked it up and began to read.

The radiation treatments ultimately proved ineffective against the lung cancer, and she was admitted to a Cleveland hospital for further evaluation. One night Holly called. "Jacq, the doctor's transferred Mom from the main hospital to Hanna Pavilion," she said.

"What!" Hanna Pavilion was the psychiatric ward of Cleveland's University Hospitals, the "loony bin," as my mother would have called it.

"Her behavior is erratic, and she's acting violent." Holly's voice quivered. "I don't know . . . she . . . They seem to think she's psychotic."

"Hol, that's impossible!" My mother had often been irritable and had occasionally seemed on the edge of a nervous breakdown, but she was not psycho. Alarmed, I arranged to fly back home once more and advised David he should plan to as well.

Marian, Holly and I visited her at Hanna Pavilion where she had been sequestered in an odd little dormered room with yellow walls. She flailed about on the bed, her speech breathy and rambling. Panic shot through me. She didn't seem to know who we were.

It was the following day I had the "metastasized" conversation with the doctor as I sat in Mom's living room. He made no reference to his misstep in committing her to the psych ward; instead he fumbled with his medical jargon to inform me the cancer had spread from her lungs to her brain. The hospital could do nothing for her and was sending her home to die.

So, it was brain cancer that was causing her bizarre behavior. I was relieved to know my mother hadn't gone insane, but fearful about what dying of a brain tumor might mean.

We immediately made arrangements for round-the-clock nurses to be at her bedside, administer her morphine and provide whatever care she needed as soon as she got home. I comforted myself with the thought that dying in her own house rather than in the hospital would be my mother's wish.

The next morning the ambulance arrived at the house. The attendants carried my mother's frail form on a stretcher through our spidery, leaf-litter-strewn garage, muscling it up the dark narrow steps between the lower levels, then up another flight to her bedroom. Following this arduous ordeal, we all—Marian, Holly, David, and I—huddled outside our mother's bedroom as the nurse dressed her in the flannel Lanz nightgown we'd laid out. When we tiptoed back in, her flimsy smile and the breathless delight she seemed to express at being home in her own bed offered us some relief.

"Never heard of such a thing! Never heard of such a thing!" she said in a wild, whispery voice. This familiar expression of hers gave me a glimmer of hope that perhaps the doctors were wrong, perhaps she would be herself again. Holly and I tried to call her attention to the Valentine cards and get-well wishes we had taped onto her dressing table mirror. But "Never heard of such a thing! Never heard of such a thing!" was all she said.

Once the ambulance crew had gone and my mother was settled in, I explained to the nurse as much as I understood about her condition and the cause of her erratic behavior. The woman's gawking expression told me she had no experience caring for a brain cancer patient. Nevertheless, she returned to my mother's bedroom to perform her required duties.

That afternoon, like four small children, Holly, Marian, David and I stood at our mother's bedside as she moaned and thrashed. Suddenly she became aware of our hovering presence, and with all the strength she could muster, she cried, "Get out! Go away! Just get out!"

Stunned, we slunk away to other parts of the house. I attributed her outburst to the cancer eating away at her brain and perhaps to her need for privacy, but all the same the rebuke hurt like hell.

It was impossible to know if, under the influence of morphine, she was rational or not. Was she hallucinating? Being driven wild by pain? Or did she just not want us near her? But if she was rational, why was she spurning us, when we were there to try to offer comfort?

Later I realized it had always been so. She had never accepted solace from her children. Our offers of help had always been rejected, like the day years ago when she'd insisted on putting up the Christmas tree by herself—"Mom, can we help?" "No, dear, it's all right about me, I can manage." She had always pushed us away as though she feared relying on us. As though accepting our support would somehow be admitting defeat.

When I tiptoed back into my mother's bedroom, I cringed at her cries, her moans, and her struggle with what seemed a tangled net of mental and physical torment. She tugged violently at her nightgown, yanking it high above her waist, revealing her pale, emaciated nakedness. This near-cadaver, stretched to its limits in agony, was all that remained of the strong, tanned mother I'd always known. And the one thing she'd dreaded—the pain—she had not been spared.

With nothing for them to do, David and Marian departed for her house, and Holly and I stayed. We fidgeted around, walking back and forth from room to room, trying to occupy ourselves with some task—scrubbing the kitchen counter, straightening bookshelves, dusting the piano—anything to distract us from our mother's misery.

I opened the refrigerator door and found cans of spoiled sauces, moldy bread, and several jars of currant jelly she'd bought having forgotten she already had one. I pulled the foul food from the shelves and pitched it into the garbage. She wouldn't be needing any currant jelly now.

Knowing the end was near, I realized I had no idea what to do when Mom died— who do I call? Where does she get buried? I was at a total loss and could only think to call Ken. Though he and I were in the final stages of our painful separation, and I had never been in the habit of asking him for help, he was the only person I could turn to. His mother had recently died; he'd know what to do.

"I don't know what I'm supposed to do!" I sobbed openly; hiding my emotions from him no longer made sense. "What happens when she's dead, who do I call?"

"Don't worry, here's what you have to think about. . ." Ken took charge and in an uncommonly sympathetic way, led me through the steps of deciding on a funeral home; he explained what assistance they'd provide us when the time came. I wondered why I had never come to rely on his help throughout our marriage. Why did it take a state of desperate need to get me to open myself to him?

The next afternoon, on the instruction of the nurse—she had become surly dealing with her raving patient—I drove to the drug store to renew Mom's morphine prescription. I waited for what seemed like hours as the pharmacist phoned the doctor to straighten out a technical flaw in the writing of the scrip. Fear and frustration seared through my body as I shifted my weight from one foot to the other.

Finally, craning my neck to see what was taking so long with the pharmacist, I screamed at the clerk, "Can't you hurry? My mother's in pain! She's dying! I have to have that medicine NOW!" Other store customers waiting in line looked away, as if they would rather be anywhere else. A woman pulled her little girl away from the counter. At last I grabbed the little white paper bag and ran out into the cold.

That evening a blustery snowstorm developed. The night nurse failed to arrive for her shift. When I phoned her, she insisted that because of the heavy snow, she wouldn't be able to get to us. She was just plain not coming. The nurse on duty turned to me.

"It's the end of my shift. I gotta get home."

"No," I cried, "you can't leave us! We don't know what to do!" The panic in my voice scared me.

"I gotta get home," she said, her deep brown eyes pleading. She must have feared she wouldn't be able to get her car out of our icy driveway and find her way to Cleveland through the snow if she stayed a minute longer. She administered my mother's dose of morphine, gave us some cursory instructions, and left.

Holly and I looked at each other in bewilderment; we were way out of our element. Nothing in our upbringing had prepared us for sitting by the bedside of our dying mother. We had no experience in ministering to the sick. We knew nothing of nurturing care. We sat on either side of our mother's bed and tried to think what we should do.

Only the dim hallway light illuminated the bedroom. We sat in near darkness as my mother thrashed from side to side, moaning and whimpering like an injured dog. She had no idea we were close by. Holly sat on one edge of the bed and placed a cool washcloth on her brow. From a low armchair at the other side of the bed I took her hand in mine, supposing that was what one did in this circumstance. As I sat there, my face flushed with fear, I realized: I'd never before held my mother's hand.

The physical contact felt awkward. Hugs had always been uncommon in our family, and kisses were delivered into the air close by a person's ear or skipped altogether. But now, in the calm of night, I held her frail hand, then began to caress it, stroking the delicate flesh, bones so close to the surface. I shushed her groans and sat through the endless hours without uttering a word. I wondered if I was to be witness to my mother's death. I dreaded seeing her demise but, at the same time, yearned for her release from torture.

My mother didn't die that night. She rallied the next day; she ate a bit of orange Jello. A nurse finally arrived. After much inner struggle, I decided to head back to Connecticut to take care of work at the office before the end came. Three days later, the day after Valentine's Day, I got the call from Holly at two a.m. Our mother was gone. I flew back home to be with my brother and sisters.

We gathered at Marian's to mourn our loss. We had many drinks. We all lit cigarettes—though Holly and I had never smoked—and puffed away and soaked our feelings in alcohol. A peculiar tribute to our mom, a futile attempt to stay connected to her. And then I felt it. The huge void in the room. There was someone missing. A big someone. The jokester, the complainer, the martyr, the manipulator. Absent. Lost.

We shed no tears that night. Our family does not weep at death. We merely accept and move on. That is our way.

A month later we had a memorial service for our mother at St. Christopher's followed by a small gathering of friends at the house for drinks and food. After the guests left, Marian, David, Holly, and I all got mildly drunk, our lonely and exhausted bodies strewn around the living room furniture. My cousin Jeanie was there, too.

All of a sudden Holly flew into a rage. "We killed her!" she cried, "*We* killed her!" My heart stopped. "We disappointed her!" she screamed, her face red with tears and wrath. "We were never the children she wanted us to be!"

David, discarding his sardonic shell, put his arms around Holly and with uncharacteristic tenderness assured her she was wrong. "Mom was killed by cigarettes and liquor," he told her, "not by us." The rest of us rushed to agree. "That's right, Hol, it was the cigarettes!

And all that drinking." We reassured Holly she hadn't been killed by us.

"Not us," I murmured trying to calm my little sister, "not us." Though, in the back of my mind, a doubt lurked. My failed marriage, I thought. Could her disappointment over my pending divorce have contributed to her anxiety—and to her death?

It was fully a year later that I confronted the loss of my mother. I had managed to keep my feelings at bay till then by focusing on practical matters regarding her estate. While Holly did the bulk of the work dealing with our mother's various banks, I attended to the distribution of her belongings, the sale of the house; they were nuts and bolts details I was good at managing but held little connection to the loss of a loved one.

A year after her death, however, on a bright February day, I glanced at a photo on my guest-room dresser, a picture of my mother feeding pigeons in a piazza in Rome on one of her trips with Uncle Minkie. She looked so happy in that moment, a wary smile on her face, a squint in her eye, holding crumbs for those pigeons. I could imagine her chuckling as the birds cooed and careened around her, pecking at her open palm.

Then it struck me like a dull sword. I would never again hear my mother's laugh. I would never see her rugged face, never again enjoy one of her smart-aleck remarks. That complex, difficult woman, who, in her distinctive and imperfect fashion, had steered me through life, had vanished. And my memories of her, I realized with dismay, were already slipping away like trickles of water over a craggy falls.

My eyes stung. I slumped onto the bed and let the tears flow. With my cheek enveloped in the soft texture of the patchwork quilt,

I cried, "Mommy, where are you?" My fingers tore at the fabric. "I want my Mom!"

"She died with as much difficulty as she lived," said my sister Marian. It seemed our mother's life had been one struggle after another, despite having been wealthy and educated. And her difficulties had been imprinted onto her children, stamped onto our psyches— mine, at least—for all time.

But my mother's anxious childhood, her stressful adolescence, and her bitter divorce, were not the whole story. Something else, a hidden element that may have fueled her unhappiness and her quirky temperament, was yet to be revealed.

19
DAD—PART TWO

With Mom gone, I was down to one parent. I had seen less and less of my father since our childhood jaunts to his house at Tuckaway. Sunday visits had petered out and been replaced by Christmas get-togethers and occasional dinners with him and Polly. But later, when they had moved to Chatham on Cape Cod and I was living in Connecticut, our geographical closeness provided an opportunity for me to get to know him better.

I'd always wondered if my mother's on-going complaints about my father had been justified. Maybe, I thought, her bitter words against him had obligated us to keep him at arm's length. And maybe he'd sidestepped some of his paternal responsibilities because he suspected she'd hardened us against him. Now that my mother was gone, I thought, I could work to develop a relationship with him without feeling disloyal to her. Maybe my father had never been given a fair chance.

The year my mother died, I'd been studying landscape design and was on my way to earning a certificate degree, with the hopes of starting a new career. After completing my studies, successfully designing some projects for a landscape firm, and giving the idea much careful thought, I worked up the nerve to launch my own design business. My mother, especially at the Chesterland house, had become an avid gardener, so I knew she'd have approved of my plan. I wasn't so sure about my father's reaction, but I had warm memories of the time Dad and I had laid a brick patio together and planted pink geraniums around the pool at his Chatham house. I phoned him to share my excitement at becoming an entrepreneur.

"Hey, Dad, guess what! I'm setting up my very own landscape design business!" Silence met my cheery news.

"Dad?" Maybe he hadn't heard me.

"But, dear," he finally asked, "do you know anything about landscape design?"

His question stunned me. He had to know I'd been studying design. Did he think I was the sort of person who'd embark on a career without any qualifications? Why would he want to deflate my enthusiasm with such a remark?

It reminded me of an incident years before when I'd been home from college and Dad had asked me what I planned to do when I graduated. I'd dreaded his asking, as his reaction could only be negative. But I decided to come out with it. "Well, actually, Dad," I cleared my throat, "I want to be an actress."

"Oh, no, Jacq!" he laughed, his sharp teeth gleaming. "You can't do that! You should be a secretary. Something like that, something solid."

Ouch, worse than I'd feared. He knew I'd played lead roles in teen theatre musicals, and that I was immersed in drama at college. He didn't always attend my performances—in fact he missed most of them—but I assumed he recognized my talent and knew acting was my first love. His suggestion I should be a secretary made me wince. How could his expectations for me be so low?

Now, twenty years later, his reaction to my new design career left me with the same bitter taste of discouragement. I hung up the phone feeling exasperated.

I did launch my landscape business, however, and it took off like an eager young sapling. On one visit to Chatham I looked forward to impressing my father with success stories of designing gardens and managing clients. However, he never asked about my business. And I never piped up to boast of my accomplishments. Instead I spent the afternoon yanking at a mass of invasive English ivy that threatened to devour the cedar shingles of his house.

One day Polly, who for years had suffered from back pain and heart problems, had a severe stroke. She was admitted to a nursing home that offered very fine care, and Dad visited her faithfully every day. Not long after, though, he had a mild stroke himself and hired a professional caretaker to cook for him, pay his bills, and shuttle him back and forth to the nursing home.

Thinking he might be lonely, I drove up to Chatham to see him on a regular basis. But he began to dodge my visits and make excuses why I shouldn't come.

"Dear, it's going to rain this weekend. Maybe you should visit another time," he said over the phone.

Disappointed, I countered with, "But, Dad, I can drive in the rain."

"No, you better not come. It's not safe." Puzzled, I abandoned my plan.

After years in the nursing home Polly weakened and died. I again tried to lend my father support with calls and cheery visits. I drove up to the Cape, thinking he'd enjoy having some time with his daughter, only to find him utterly pre-occupied with something quite unexpected: his girlfriend, Simone. A bossy, hard-haired septuagenarian dedicated to maintaining a youthful social schedule, Simone was intent on keeping Dad busy by dragging him to cocktail parties, dinner dances, and trips to the beach.

Around this time, my father came to describe himself as the "nervous type." I took that as a warning of sorts that I should avoid discussion of anything hinting at bad news. So, though I was going through a very rough time with my mother gone and my marriage in ruins, I never told him Ken and I had separated, fearing he'd be unnerved by such a failure. And I never mentioned a word about my divorce. Though Marian or Holly must have passed on that information to him, he never asked me about it.

However, when George became such an important person in my life, I felt this good news would be acceptable, perhaps even welcome. So I took my boyfriend up to Chatham to meet my dad. Having suffered a more serious stroke by that time, my father was ensconced in his den on a ragged upholstered easy chair set in front of a card table and TV. I leaned over to give him a kiss on the cheek.

"Hi, dear." His short silver hair was disheveled; his voice sounded uncommonly weak.

"How are you doing, Dad?"

"Not so well, dear. I can't see, can barely read the paper."

I was eager to reveal the purpose of my visit. "Dad, this is my friend George!"

My father glanced in George's direction and, without greeting him or shaking his hand, said in hardy tones, "George, you seem like a strong fellow." He gestured to a window at his side. "Could you pull up this stubborn storm window for me?" Eager to please,

George struggled with a window that had been set crookedly in its frame.

"And, Jacq, could you go down to the liquor store and get me a bottle of gin? And a couple of nips for Simone. Just put it on my account."

The rest of our visit revolved around taking my father out to lunch, attending to his errands and chores, and delivering him and Simone to the beach. We dropped them off at the edge of the sandy parking lot.

"You OK, Dad?" I questioned his ability to cope with such an activity.

"Yes, yes, dear. See you later."

As I looked back, my father, feeling his way with his cane, staggered beneath the weight of a beach chair slung over his shoulder as he trailed after Simone onto the dunes.

In a matter of months, complications from Dad's stroke forced him to move to the nursing home, where he remained for the rest of his life. Holly, Marian, David and I visited him often, usually to deliver his Christmas or birthday gifts. We wandered through hallways cluttered with wheelchairs and laundry bags to find his room. Dad, having injured his ankle, refused to leave his bed and was determined to be permanently bedridden. We struggled to keep up a conversation with him, an exchange much hampered by his slurred speech and failing eyesight.

"How are you doing, Dad?" I asked with forced cheer. I leaned over the edge of his bed to intercept his line of vision, nearly upsetting the plastic urinal suspended from the bed rail. "Are the nurses taking good care of you?" His vacuous stare informed me he had no particular interest in our being there.

But, in spite of his infirmities, my father was determined to play the role of jokester, making caustic remarks about the nursing home staff and other residents. "Old woman came in last night," he said one day in a hoarse, chirpy voice. "Crept into my room late. Into my bathroom. Stole my Listerine! Ha-ha!" We all tittered, unsure if he was making a joke or had suffered a midnight delusion.

My last photos of my father propped up in his nursing home bed capture him making bizarre faces at the camera. His deliberately contrived grimaces of lunacy, sturdy yellow teeth clenched, silver-blue eyes bugging out of their sockets—attempts, perhaps, to amuse—fill almost every shot. Joke or delusion? Why couldn't our father pose without making grotesque faces? I wondered. Why couldn't he let his children have even one normal photo? Why was he hiding?

My father's weakened state had inserted a new element into my relationship with him. At the end of every phone call or weekend visit he was quick to say, "I love you, dear." A declaration I'd never heard from my father over the course of forty years, it stunned and nettled me. It sounded so hollow. "I love you, too, Dad," I murmured—the only possible response. The words felt like dust on my tongue.

When my father's condition eventually deteriorated and he was near death, my brother David spent long hours at his bedside to make sure he received proper care up till the end, but I myself felt no such obligation. By then I'd come to feel ministering to my father was, at best, a thankless task.

The year following his death, I read the diaries he'd left behind—from the years when Polly was in the nursing home and he was living alone. Perusing with care the weathered daily calendars, I found in his cramped handwriting little mention of any of his children—almost none. Though we had called and visited him often, it appeared we were very much on the periphery of his life, barely a footnote.

When my mother used to tell us my dad was "rotten," I'd always assumed she meant he was rotten to *her*. But she may, in fact, have been alerting us to something quite different. She may have been warning us that he was so self-absorbed he was incapable of providing anything for her *or* for his children.

My efforts, then, to create some sort of fond relationship with my father after my mother's death were futile—silly, actually. How could I have been so shortsighted? When I'd reached to him for paternal affection, he simply didn't have it to give.

20

THE ACCIDENT

A few days after my mother's death our Uncle Dick, who was executor of her will, came to the Chesterland house to discuss legal matters with Holly and me. Uncle Dick, our mother's older brother—the one whose accomplishments she'd felt as a child she could never measure up to—was nearly a stranger. He and my mother had not been terribly close, and when I was a little girl, his ragged eyebrows, big teeth, and steely smile used to make me squirm. But on this day I stared at Uncle Dick as we sat around the dining room table and he told us a remarkable story.

We had always known that my mother and father had been in a car crash before they were married. My mother often complained her looks had been destroyed by that accident, her jaw smashed, her teeth knocked out of alignment.

According to people who knew her before the tragic incident, she had been a beautiful girl. A photographic portrait of her from about age eighteen captures a slender, sophisticated young woman with a slightly upturned nose. Around her neck, above the lace collar of her velvet dress, hangs a gold filigree necklace. Her dark hair is drawn back from her face. Her mouth bears no hint of a smile. Her eyes hold deep sadness.

From my viewpoint as a child, my mother had been a good-looking woman, tall with sturdy bones. Her fingers were blunt, her hands strong, her skin perpetually tanned. To me the extra lines on her face and her slightly crooked teeth were signs of character. Still, the plaint, "That accident destroyed my face and wrecked my life," was what we heard as we were growing up.

What she did not tell us was the story Uncle Dick divulged to Holly and me that day, when I asked him to describe the details of the accident. His salt-and-pepper eyebrows lifted in surprise at our ignorance of it.

"Well, it was a nasty head-on collision on a winding road out in Willoughby. Your mother and father were on their way to a party. Oh, it was a terrible smashup. Both cars were pretty much demolished. Fortunately, our sister—your Auntie Marian—was following your mother's car in hers. When she saw the crash, she jumped from her car and somehow managed to drag your mother out of the smoking wreck. Your father was barely conscious—he'd suffered a concussion, I think—so Marian was the only one who could pull your mother out. If she hadn't, your mother might have died in that wreck."

Uncle Dick looked from me to Holly and back again. "You didn't know about this?"

We sat agog, never having guessed that Auntie Marian had saved our mother's life. All we knew of Auntie Marian was that—according to my mother—she'd been the beautiful, talented daughter of the family, she had occasionally sung in nightclubs when she was young, and she drank herself to death after the loss of her husband.

The revelation that she'd pulled her sister out of a car wreck and saved her life gave our Auntie Marian a whole new dimension.

As I was seeing Uncle Dick to the door, I felt the need to make some mention of Mamama, since she was the link to him. "We have fond recollections of her," I said, "we miss her."

"Who, Mamama?" he asked. "Oh, she was a terrible person. Bossiest woman alive, always telling us what to do, never giving us a moment's peace—"

I was nearly speechless at this description of our elegant grandmother. "Well, I know she did manage to give my mother sort of an inferiority complex—"

"Oh, she did that to all of us! If she was talking to Jean and me, all we heard was how beautiful Marian was. And Marian and I had to hear all about Jean's wondrous accomplishments. And my sisters probably got an earful about how brilliant I was. That's what they did in those days. Praise your siblings, so you wouldn't get a swelled head. We all ended up with complexes." He chuckled wryly and turned to leave. I said thank you and goodbye to my uncle, pondering this eye-opening news.

After Uncle Dick had enlightened us about the accident, I gave it little more thought, until one day I took a closer look at the photograph of my sister Marian's christening. I studied the scars and lines around my mother's mouth and her curious lack of a smile. I compared it to the coquettish grin on Auntie Marian's face, and I realized my aunt must have been acting as the baby's godmother on that day, and the child had of course been named after her.

Then in 2001, sixteen years after my mother's death, new information about the accident surfaced. Following my father's death in 1999, my sister Marian, a history professor and an inveterate researcher, decided to read through the copious hand-written diaries of our Grandpa, Dad's father. There she found several entries with references to the car accident and some sort of legal settlement pertaining to it. She decided to dig further and unearthed two newspaper articles from 1936. One day I received in the mail a thick envelope from Marian.

"*Dear Jacq*," she wrote in her letter, "*Enclosed are two articles about the accident . . . Some scary stuff!*" I unfolded the Xerox copies of the sixty-five year old articles. A headline shimmered before my eyes.

SOCIETY COUPLE IS INJURED IN
WEDDING EVE CRASH

My eyes skipped down to the photo of a breezy debutante wearing dangling earrings and a cocky smile, my mother. She had indeed been stunning. Then I read the article text:

> *Miss Jean Inglis, 22, socially prominent bride-*
> *to-be and her fiancé David L. Johnson, Jr., 23,*
> *lay critically injured in Lakeside Hospital today*
> *while their wedding, scheduled for Thursday, was*
> *postponed indefinitely.*

I blinked in amazement. The crash had happened just days before my parents' wedding date. But there was more to the headline—something I'd skipped over. I went back.

SOCIETY COUPLE IS INJURED IN
WEDDING EVE CRASH
AS OTHER DRIVER DIES

A thumping filled my chest. I stared at the paper without seeing, as blood rushed through my skull. What *was* this? I returned to the text.

> *In the same accident, a head-on automobile*
> *collision near Willoughby, John Martin, 37,*
> *manager of the Lake County airport, was injured*
> *so severely he died five hours later."*

The article went on to say the dead man was survived by a wife and four children. I tried to grasp what I was reading, but the words were blurred and shifting back and forth on the page.

I turned to the second article, published a day later. It reported the society couple was recovering nicely. And it gave notice of the dead man's funeral arrangements. Further on, the story revealed my mother's car had caused the crash. Sheriff's deputies' investigation of skid marks had shown her car to be two feet over the centerline of the road for 150 feet before impact with the other automobile. Who the driver of her car had been was unclear. *"The deputies,"* the article stated, *"said they had not determined who was driving the Inglis car."*

This was devastating. How on earth could I not know of this catastrophe? I turned back to Marian's accompanying letter. She made no other mention of the tragic accident. Her note went on—perhaps in an attempt to mitigate the startling news of the articles—to describe what she'd read in Grandpa's diaries about his social life in Cleveland and the various failings of his four children.

I looked up from the letter and articles, unable or unwilling to fully digest their contents. There must be some mistake, I thought. The newspapers must have had our parents confused with another couple. If this had really happened, how could I not know about it? But the newspaper headlines stared up at me. The two articles with photos of my parents couldn't be wrong. I re-read them two or three times, seeking to refute the words on the page. I could make no sense of any of it. I stashed the papers in my desk drawer and puzzled over how this secret had been kept from us.

Later I pieced together the story—two young socialites speeding along a winding road on their way to a party, a horrible crash, a debutante saving her sister's life, a dead man in the other car, the marriage of two guilty people, the bitter end of that marriage, the death of the courageous sister, and the raising of orphaned cousins. A series of jagged links defining the framework of our family.

My mother had chosen, not surprisingly, to withhold the details of the accident from her children. She never told us her sister had saved her life. She never told us a man had been killed. She told us only about the mangling of her face and how it had ruined her life.

But how did this dreadful accident sculpt my mother's adulthood? Did carrying that terrible secret inside her contribute to her drinking and distracted behavior? Or not? Did she continually lament the horrifying event? Or dismiss it as youthful carelessness? Did she often revisit the terrifying images of the collision? Or had she forgotten them altogether?

When she focused on her own visage, still bearing the scars of that day, how did my mother see herself? And how did it feel to carry such a secret within her for so many years?

The answers to these questions are missing pieces of the puzzle that was my mother. Exactly what went on in her heart and mind we will never know, as she shared so little of her deepest thoughts. And unfortunately she has handed down no written word to explain herself to us. She has left behind only her children—the products of her idiosyncratic, self-styled mothering—to attempt to tell the tale.

21

FOUND

Where else, I wonder with a growing sense of desperation, where else can I find something, anything at all, written in my mother's distinctive hand? Once again I scan around my untidy home office for places I might have stored any letters from her. Coming up empty, I call Marian to ask if she has any samples of my mother's handwriting, as I am, for some reason, anxious to lay my eyes on it. Marian mails me a Xerox copy of a scrap of paper that says "Marian," probably a homemade gift tag from a long-forgotten Christmas present. That's all she could find. Not helpful.

Finally I give up searching. With a landscape design business to run, I have plenty of other things pressing for my attention. Maybe the letters will turn up, but most likely they are lost forever.

Then one day, out of the blue, it hits me—the Journal Box. My mother's letters could be in there.

When my marriage to Ken was collapsing, the first thing I did was begin to write, setting down with pencil and paper all the feelings that beset me—disappointment, betrayal, anger and fear. I made lists, wrote paragraphs, and composed long missives to myself detailing what was coursing through my brain and my fractured heart. I wrote down all the insights I was acquiring with my therapist, catalogued the pain and confusion, and struggled to make sense of my husband's hurtful behavior and my failure as a wife. I vented feelings I'd never expressed, either as I was growing up or in my marriage.

In the process of all this journaling—my emotional outpouring could only be scribbled down with pen or pencil—a huge amount of paper piled up. Later I transferred most of the writing onto my computer and created an inch-thick printout. But I neurotically held on to the original pencil drafts, as well as other longhand pages I generated almost daily. To accommodate all this paper, well beyond what would fit in any notebook, I found a large, square cardboard hatbox. I tossed my journal entries, roughly in chronological order, and the typed manuscript into this box, scrawled "My Journal" across the top, and put it aside.

Over the next few years I focused on my burgeoning landscape design career. Managing that enterprise had begun to consume me and allowed little time for soul searching and writing prose. The hatbox, which eventually got buried on a musty corner of my reference table under plans and sketches of gardens and landscape features, was nearly forgotten.

The Journal Box—that's it! Excited, I extract the box from beneath the pile of drawings, brush gritty dust from its top, and lift the lid. I pull out a grimy manila folder entitled "Poetry and Papers—J.J." and an assortment of journal entries on lined yellow paper. And there they are—note cards from my mother. These must be the letters she had written when I was having such a miserable time separating from Ken, and I'd stashed them away with all my journaling.

I stare at one of the note cards, the front of which is a romantic painting of snow-capped mountains, a river, a cliff, dark trees, and a flood of light streaming through stormy clouds. I open the card. There in my mother's lovely loopy italics I read,

> *Dearest Jackie,*
> *I feel as if I were trying to communicate from*
> *the insides of a brown paper bag—knowing so*
> *little of what's going on there.*

She must have written this letter the day after I had called her to break the news about my separation from Ken. I had kept that conversation short, as I feared hostile comments toward him, her bitter words only increasing my sadness. I had made my account of our separation sketchy and asked her not to phone me, insisting I was working things out on my own.

> *Whatever it is, she wrote, I'm with you all*
> *the way and wish desperately that I could do*
> *something, anything, to help you. Please let me*
> *know if anything comes up, day or night, in which*
> *I can be of any comfort.*
> *You are a splendid person and among your*
> *enviable qualities are intelligence and a clear-*
> *headed thoughtfulness, so it's very likely that*
> *advice may not be what you need. I feel that all I*
> *can do is be here if you want to talk about things.*

I am surprised by her faith in my ability to cope in the face of trouble. And I am astonished that my mother thought I was a splendid person.

> *I'll try not to call you, since it is hard for you now*
> *to talk about things. But do enlighten me when*
> *you feel up to it.*
>   *I love you, Jackie, and am eager to do anything*
> *I can for you. God bless you.*

Mom

Warm tears spill down my cheeks, trail along my jawbone, and trickle down my neck. I re-read her words, then turn back to the scene on the front of the note card. Brilliant sun is piercing through dark billowing clouds, a detail I'd not noticed when I'd originally read the letter twenty-four years before. Though perhaps she had.

I lift the next note card depicting an idealized rustic scene and open it. My mother has written her predictable description of relentless snowfall and unendurable temperatures in wintry Chesterland and adds,

> *I don't know who thought up that wind chill*
> *business. It just makes everything seem worse.*

She also recounts news of a visit from Uncle Dick and the activities of various grandchildren, then,

> *All this is very boring. I'm really dropping a*
> *line so you'll know we're all thinking about you,*
> *and praying that whatever is best for you will*
> *come about. We're all behind you, and Holly*
> *and/or I, at least, can come there if you should*
> *want us. In the meantime, we go our little ways*
> *not happily, perhaps, but hopefully. I have not*
> *mentioned your troubles to anyone except the*
> *family as I feel you may be more comfortable not*
> *having them a subject of general discussion.*

These cards are awful to write on. The ink just
slithers around.

Hang in there.

Loads of love,

Mom

I grin at her ink comment and pause to grab a Kleenex to wipe my cheeks and blow my nose. I read through the other note cards, six in all, each one ending in "Hang in there," and place them with care into the oversized hatbox.

Then I catch sight of a small battered piece of paper I've over-looked. I unfold it. It's a letter from my mother, apparently when she was gravely ill.

Please do not worry about me. God has
always been, without any merit on my part, very
good to me, and I see no reason why he won't
continue to be.

Mrs. Moatz is coming over soon to take me to
her house for lunch, which will be fun. I have a lot
of good friends.

Much love as always,

Mom

This note, written on a dog-eared scrap of lined paper, must have been the last letter my mother ever wrote me.

How on earth could I have forgotten about these note cards? How could the memory of their message have escaped me? And how could I have failed to remember that, in spite of all else, she did try to be a loving mother?

But I have to ask myself, what other expressions of love and admiration did our mother withhold from her children? And for what reason?

There is a story about my mother that has often been told in our family and modified according to who's repeating it. It seems she was giving a large dinner party at the West Hill Drive house, a party for her gourmet cooking club.

My mother was many things, but she was not a gourmet cook. Her culinary specialty when Holly and I were growing up was spaghetti casserole, a blend of hamburger, onion, cream of tomato soup, and Velveeta cheese. Nevertheless she was fond of trying new things, so she joined a friend's gourmet club, invited several guests, and found a recipe she felt worthy, artichoke hearts and white wine being its exotic ingredients. Then she bought an enormous earthenware casserole dish in which to cook and serve it.

On the evening of the dinner party Holly and I, about eight and ten at the time, were in the kitchen helping her, while her guests sat at the formal dining room table. My mother pulled the casserole out of the oven, removed the lid, poked her finger into it to test for doneness, and said, "Stand back, girls, I'm going to carry this through the pantry into the dining room."

Holly and I stared at the concoction; it seemed yucky to us with its foreign ingredients. We moved out of her way as with two shabby potholders she lifted the huge piping-hot casserole. She staggered uncertainly through the kitchen towards the butler's pantry. But the enormous dish was too hot and too heavy to handle. Before she could reach the pantry counter for support, the immense casserole slipped from her hands and crashed to the floor, its contents and crockery combined into one steaming heap. Holly and I groaned. My mother, close to tears, swung the pantry door to the dining room shut.

One of the guests, having heard the sound of potential calamity, called in, "Jean, everything all right in there? Can we help?"

"No, no, no thanks! The children are helping me!" she answered with the breeziest tone she could muster.

The three of us stared at the oozing pile of what looked like the vomit of a giant. Knowing there was no other food to serve and no take-out restaurants to call, my mother whispered frantically, "Quick, children, help me scrape this up! Just pick out the crockery as you go."

"But, Mom—!"

"It'll be fine! Just fine."

She found another casserole, less glamorous than the first, and we scooped up the artichoke hearts and other bits of ingredients from the floor, avoiding the shattered crockery as best we could. Within moments we pulled the meal together, and my mother swept through the pantry door carrying her exotic, albeit luke-warm, gourmet dish. Holly and I stayed behind in the pantry with our ears to the door, as the clatter of plates, utensils, and dinner table chit-chat began.

"Jean, dear, this is delicious!" someone said amidst the clinking of crockery bits on plates. Her friends, too polite to mention the chunks of earthenware they were encountering, dined away. "*Where* did you find this recipe?" Clink. Clink. The dinner party proceeded.

While everyone in our family screams with laughter whenever they hear the casserole story, it pains me now to think how crushed with embarrassment my mother might have been, knowing the main event of her gala dinner party had been a debacle. It pains me, because that is how I would have felt if it had been my party, and I am my mother's daughter. I envision her lying awake late that night after her friends had gone home, recalling the crashing of her gour-met masterpiece to the floor. I picture her tossing and turning as the image of guests discreetly picking crockery from their teeth replays in her head again and again. I can hear her castigating herself for botching her much-anticipated dinner party.

Imagining her feelings at such a moment, her possible anguish, makes me wish I could put my arms around my mother and pull her close to me and tell her it's all right. This is something I never did in real life, take her in my arms, but I am able do it now in my mind's eye. *It's OK, Mom, it's not important,* I tell her. *The dinner party was fun anyway, Mom, everybody had a good time, the evening was a success.*

In my imaginary scene I hold her in a firm embrace. And she allows me to. She doesn't push me away and say, "Never mind, it's all right about me." She accepts my gesture of comfort. She relaxes into my arms. And I hold her and rock her back and forth, feeling her soft flesh and sturdy bones tight up against my own.

As I pull my mother to me, I am, in a sense, embracing myself. So much of her lives on in me: intense self-absorption, random irritability, craving for solitude, stubborn self-reliance, and on and on. I am my mother. Every fiber of my being holds her deficiencies. I must accept and embrace them—along with the worthy qualities she possessed —for she was all I had.

In my fantasy, I press her close to me, and I assure her everything's OK. *Don't worry, Mom, it all worked out. We're all fine. Everything is fine, Mom, just fine.*

And we are fine. Jeanie and Susan are both well. And each of us four kids—Marian, David, Holly and I—are fine, too. We've had productive, satisfying lives and have profited from the sound values our mother passed along to us. Apart from occasional losses, ailments, and upsets of one sort or another, each of us is strong, healthy and prosperous.

As testament to our good fortune, on any given day, each of us can be found in our respective homes, sitting in a comfortable chair, reading a book. Marian in her Cleveland Heights bungalow, David in his simple house in Greenwich, Holly in her lovely home in Chagrin Falls, and I in my Connecticut country cottage. Reading a good book.